Watch for more books from Susan Emmerich
from Second Wind Publishing

www.secondwindpublishing.com

A Girl on a Bike

Musings on Life, Loss, and Hot Flashes

By

Susan Emmerich

Sandpiper Books
Published by Second Wind Publishing, LLC.
Kernersville

Sandpiper Books
Second Wind Publishing, LLC
931-B South Main Street, Box 145
Kernersville, NC 27284

First Sandpiper Books edition published
January, 2015.
Sandpiper Books, Running Angel, and all production design are
trademarks of Second Wind Publishing, used under license.

For information regarding bulk purchases of this book, digital
purchase and special discounts, please contact the publisher at
www.secondwindpublishing.com

Cover design by Todd Engel

Manufactured in the United States of America
ISBN 978-1-63066-123-6

For my father, Mike Emmerich, who gave me wings.
For my daughter, Julie Jensen, who is my reason to fly.

ACKNOWLEDGEMENTS

A book is never written by just one person, and this is no exception. My ideas and words would never have come together without the support and wisdom of others. The inspiration for many of the essays is my family: Ann Emmerich, Bob Emmerich, Nancy Bolduc, Barbara Harrington, Tricia Adams, and Michael Emmerich. Our connection defines and nurtures me every day and my heart is whole because of you.

I want to thank Laura Jensen for always finding the soul of a piece. Your willingness to provide insights and recommendations taught me that words have the power to both comfort and challenge. Thanks to Sara Fagnilli for all things legal and technical and helping me keep the goal in sight. Whether it is physical or mental, you make me reach further.

To my CV sisters: Barbara Caravona, Patty Keberle, Barbara Kilker, Maria Mueller, and Suzanne Smiley-Rozic, thank you for always believing in me…more than I did in myself. You taught me that just maybe, getting pizza and wine delivered is the best way!

Thank you to Anne Maitland. Your "gnat's ass" approach to proofing confirmed all I didn't know about a well-placed comma or semi-colon. I will forever miss our early morning walks, and I've learned that when it comes to life-long friends, miles don't matter.

As much as I love words, I'm not sure I can find the right ones to thank Jim Bloor and Deirdre Richie. For more than a year, you read, re-read, and re-read again, each of these essays. You tore them down and made me build them back up, pushing me out of my comfort zone. Your daily phone calls and willingness to listen to my frustrations kept my head from exploding. Your editing skills pale in comparison to your friendship. Never once did either of you express doubt in my abilities, even when I questioned the point of it all. Your combined wisdom is reflected on each and every page. You are as much family to me as anyone with whom I share genetics.

To my strong, smart, and beautiful daughter, Julie Jensen: thank you for sharing the journey. I love you more than cake, Toby Keith, ocean beaches…

Finally, to Dr. Aaron Ellington: if I'm Dorothy, you are the Wizard. Thank you for teaching me that despite life, loss, and hot flashes, I've always possessed the strength to find my way home.

PREFACE

I love words. Despite that, I never set out to be a writer. Actually, my fear of putting words to paper played a key role in a number of career decisions. In graduate school, I chose social work over law because I feared writing briefs. Years later, I declined an invitation to a PhD program because the word "dissertation" caused night terrors! In the years I provided counseling services, I limited my writing to clinical evaluations and adoption home-studies. Pretty bland stuff. I learned I communicated best with my voice, with conversation. I thrive sitting with people and hearing their stories, and I've driven friends crazy with questions about life, hopes, and disappointments.

So, no one was more surprised than me when I began writing. In March 2010, I realized, that despite my best attempts, I was unprepared to become an "empty nester." Recently divorced and still healing, I found myself with too much time in my own head and needed to channel the ever growing accumulation of feelings. The huge changes that were occurring had stirred up a lifetime of memories, joys, regrets, and sadness.

I started by writing a weekly blog which was followed faithfully by a total of 37 people! Each week or so found me turning a memory or experience into an emotional introspection. I was surprised by the number of people who wrote to tell me they identified with my words, with my sentiments. Mostly, women who were facing transitions and making adjustments in their own lives. I set out to question myself and ended up getting answers from others.

My sister, Nancy, was the first to suggest that I write a book. I laughed her off, calling her crazy; I couldn't fathom having words to fill all those pages. What I didn't realize at the time, was, that I already had. Through the essays, I already told a story of a life lived with love, loss, and growth. I just needed to put them together. I joined a writer's group to surround myself with people more talented than I and realized that even a bad book is difficult to write.

Despite the title, this is not a book about bike riding. It IS a book about the thoughts and insights that occurred to me while I was riding. It IS a book about the questions that occur to all of us as we age and face transitions that are both normal and scary. And it IS a book about how those same transitions left me both grieving and rejoicing.

These essays tell the stories of my daughter, Julie, graduating from high school, my adjustment to being single and dating, and the illness and death of my father. In dealing with those events, I couldn't help but revisit adopting Julie, my marriage/divorce, the death of my mother Virginia, when I was four, dad's remarriage, and the physical changes that come with being 50+ years old. Each reflection came with a reminder that our lives are a collection of stories that are never really finished. We just keep adding new chapters.

They are not all heavy emotional lifting. They are lessons of acceptance and hope; of letting go and moving on; of living. Perhaps you will see threads of your own story in these pages. If so, meet me on the bike path….we have things to talk about.

CHANGES

As a teenager, I loved rearranging the furniture in my room. Without using paint, or buying new carpet or drapes, it was easy to make the room look completely different. At least I looked at it with fresh eyes. I remember the time my sister, Nancy, and I spent hours rearranging our room to hide the spill of red nail polish on peach carpet. We had just moved into the new house and had been warned NOT to use the tiny bottles on the floor. No matter where we placed the beds or dressers, that stain stood out like a burning ember. A carefully placed "Teen" magazine solved the problem for weeks, until the spot was discovered.

Despite loving to rearrange furniture, I have never accepted change easily. I find great comfort in routine, even while welcoming new experiences. I sometimes hold on to the past too tightly, limiting my growth. Personally, I prefer changes to come on my terms, in my time, and at my discretion. Still, the last few years have brought more upheaval and disruption than I could have anticipated. But since when are we given any notice that our lives are going to be turned upside down? I lived my life in such a controlled manner that I thought nothing could penetrate the guarded walls of my existence.

I alphabetized my spices. I labeled all my shoes in boxes, I rotated my towels so they would wear out evenly. I could tell you where everything in my home was located: every piece of paper, every photograph, every Christmas decoration. On the outside, my home and family looked completely ordered. Inside, changes were going on I didn't understand or even know were occurring. Slowly my marriage was falling apart, held together by the false sense of order I had created. When it came crashing down, I never saw it coming. Suddenly, the neatly organized closets were claustrophobic and I couldn't find my way out. I couldn't breathe, let alone find my shoes! It hurt to move and everywhere I looked I saw walls. That got me thinking about caterpillars, cocoons, and how they become butterflies.

In biology, this process of change is called metamorphosis. A caterpillar is just cruising along enjoying the view when all of sudden it's locked up inside a cocoon. Does the caterpillar ever see it coming? Does it know to anticipate the change? Once inside, incredible changes take place, and after the chrysalis is formed and developed, the butterfly emerges. Amazingly, the DNA of a caterpillar is exactly the same as that of the butterfly, yet it looks and operates as a completely different creature. At first it's at great risk, until after beating its wings about, it's strong enough to take off.

I have to wonder what happens to tell the caterpillar HOW to be a butterfly. Are there instructions to let the new being know how to use its wings; instructions on how to fly? And what happens to the caterpillar? Does anyone miss it? I have to believe that to go through such a complete systemic change comes with a price.

Too often I have associated that price with pain. I assume that major change means discomfort or hurt. I tend to believe that the caterpillar feels physical pain as it goes through such a dramatic transformation. How could it not? Maybe that's why it moves slowly through that first stage, knowing what is coming, and resisting the inevitable.

My daughter, Julie, is soon graduating from high school and I will be living alone for the first time in close to 25 years. She is a swimmer and I love watching her glide through the water with what I consider virtual ease. I've complained about the time involved in traveling to meets and practices, but watching her excitement was always enough payback. Recently, I watched her climb out of the pool for the last time as a member of her school team. As she looked at the board to see she had recorded her best time ever, Julie broke into a smile that brought waves of emotion to my heart. At that moment, I understood the anguish of all parents as they begin to let go.

I spent the next several hours crying and fighting feelings of panic. What will I actually do all by myself once Julie leaves for college? Will I eat alone? Watch movies alone? Only do laundry for one? Julie is going off to college to begin to figure out who she is. I'm staying home to do the same.

I can see dramatic changes coming and I can fight or learn to fly. There seems to be the potential for pain unless I can get some direction, some instruction on how to live my life as a new being. I doubt easy answers are coming. I need to be willing to trust the process, let go of the past, and embrace the potential beauty that lies ahead. Maybe, change is simply our shift in perspective; in how we view a situation. Certainly when I rearranged furniture, the view in the morning was different. When the caterpillar is able to take flight, it sees the world in a whole new way. Perhaps it's as simple as accepting the view from where we are standing.

I think I'm getting ready to break out of the cocoon and I don't know how long it will take. I can almost feel my wings beating about and I'm guessing that, like the caterpillar, I will instinctively know how to fly. If not, I know I can proceed slowly until the view is clear.

TREASURES

As I watch my daughter, Julie, navigate the college selection process, I can't help but remember her as an inquisitive 3-year old. She and I used to love taking long walks to gather "treasures" that would fill her pockets. Julie would stop and examine every stick, stone and feather. She never wanted to leave anything behind, as she felt everything had possibilities. It made me crazy and I often had to keep my mouth shut when she collected more than she could carry. This young woman's world is once again filled with wonder and new possibilities. Much like I wanted to tell Julie what to choose and what to leave behind when she was young, I want to do the same thing now. I can't.

On those long walks, there were many times that Julie would run in front of me, turning around every few yards to make sure I was still watching. Reassured, she would happily continue her journey, filling her pockets with all she discovered. Julie never got so far ahead that I felt she was unsafe or out of reach. And if she fell, I was close enough to run and gather her up and say that everything was going to be OK. I know we're supposed to let our kids fall and get up on their own, thus making them more independent. Sometimes I couldn't always do that, couldn't always watch Julie fall. There were moments I ran to make sure she was OK, ran to help her up and remind her that I had her back.

I wonder if I made a mistake. I wonder if I've given Julie all she needs to handle the world without me being around. I find myself hanging on too tightly, being less willing to let her run ahead. Soon enough, she will be out of reach and I won't be there to fix her hurt; she will have to get up on her own.

Julie recently complained to a mutual friend how I was close to crossing over into the "lunatic phase" of parenting. I think she can feel my panic. She shared she would, after all, soon be 18 and gone. My friend, the wise person he is, told Julie I must feel I was running out of time. He wondered if I might not feel I have a limited amount of time to prepare her and feel I had completed my parenting job. As a parent, it is a huge leap of faith to believe all my wisdom has been heard and is actually in her heart and head. I worry I've missed something important to tell her. How do I know for sure that she has listened? I don't.

Here is what I do know: my daughter has a beautiful soul. She sees treasures where I see junk. She sees possibility where I see limits. She still sees opportunity where I too often see risk. Could I be looking at this in the wrong light? What if Julie has heard everything? Maybe when we were gathering up sticks and feathers and rocks, I was actually teaching her about the world and all its possibilities. Perhaps I did teach her to value all of life's wonder. Her acceptance of things is so much greater than mine. Isn't that what I've hoped for? Is there anything else to say? Or is it now my turn to listen?

Julie is telling me she's ready. She's asking me to trust her ability to make good decisions, to make her own choices about what is important. Knowing her heart better than I do, my daughter also knows her own soul better. She's asking me to let her make her own mistakes and is there really any better teacher than personal experience? Even I know the answer to that question.

So, I begin to let go. I need to let Julie once again run ahead, choosing where she wants to stop, and what she puts in her pockets. I need to find a comfortable spot from which to watch. I wonder if some of those past treasures that are still under her bed will go with her. Maybe taking a few to college will be her way of turning around to make sure that I'm still watching. When she falls, and she will, Julie will know that in some way I will always be there to gather her up.

SIGNS

Last week I ran a stop sign. No big deal. It's a stupid sign in the parking lot behind my fitness club. No real traffic, no roads, just this stupid red marker. It got me thinking: how often do I ignore hints that are meant to direct or guide me? How often do I misread events or experiences designed to teach me? Probably every day. Still, there are some signs just too hard to ignore.

Several years back, when I was offered the job as a school counselor, I was hired with the understanding that I would need to complete a graduate program in guidance counseling. I was a little offended, as I had been a practicing licensed therapist for over 20 years and already completed one master's degree. Really wanting the job, I agreed. On the day I was scheduled to take the entrance exam, I found myself doubting the decision. Did I really want to take on this task? What could I possibly learn? Was I doing the right thing?

Despite the questions, I headed to the test center and as I looked for a seat, noticed a desk with a penny underneath. It was no different than a thousand other pennies I have passed by or occasionally picked up, but something drew me to that spot. Having just read a story about pennies from heaven (you know the one: someone from heaven sends you a penny to let you know they're thinking of you), I skeptically took the seat. I sat quietly thinking, thinking about that penny.

According to the story, if the penny is indeed a message, it would be minted from a year of significance. In this case, the only way the penny under my chair would have any meaning was if it were dated 1960, the year my mother died. What were the chances of that? I rolled my eyes and picked it up just to give myself a good chuckle. Yep. 1960. As I sucked in my breath and fought a tear, I gingerly placed it on the desk in front of me. I nailed the exam! I believe in signs.

Julie and I were going through a difficult mother-daughter period and I was probably being a bit unreasonable in my expectations. We were fighting about something stupid and I was cleaning to release some frustration. Nothing calms my soul like dusting and scrubbing. As I worked my way through the spare bedroom, the large round mirror attached to my grandmother Clara's dresser fell off and hit me on the shoulder. It took some

8

effort to keep it from crashing to the floor and, as I turned to secure it back in place, a family crucifix belonging to my mother, Virginia, fell off the wall and hit me on the head! Since I implicitly trust the wisdom of my ancestors I needed to figure out what these two women were trying to tell me. As startled as I was, I realized they were most likely teaming up to tell me to get a grip! I paused and was immediately reminded to not take life so seriously as the issue between Julie and I was not really significant. Quite a sign.

This never-ending journey of figuring out who I am requires me to pay attention to any number of signals. If I ignore or misread them, I can find myself feeling lost or out of sorts. If I continue to ignore some warnings, I usually get another clearer, stronger one which feels like a '2x4' to the side of my head! The resulting headache is often painful enough to make me take stock. But when I pay attention to the signs all around me, my life seems to stay in pretty good balance, I trust I'm in the right place, my instincts are in good working order.

I need to look for those indicators sent by the universe to support my natural navigation skills. Much like I rely on the knowledge that Lake Erie is north of where I live, I know there are sure clues to guide me in the right direction. They are certainly not as dramatic as the ones sent to me by my mother and grandmother but are definitely messages. A smile, a wink, a touch on the arm are all proof I'm cared for. A canceled event, a snowstorm or car trouble are all reminders that I should slow down. Song lyrics that resonate serve to remind me my dreams and struggles are not unique to me. The sound of crashing waves or a running river tell me powers greater than myself exist. How can anyone ignore new leaves or the first daffodil as signs that life really does renew itself?

I need to see directions often to keep me on the road I'm traveling. Clara's dressers have been in my home for 30 years and these elegant pieces of furniture are daily reminders of how my journey is guided by my past. Periodic wrong turns make sure I'm not moving through my present too quickly.

That 1960 penny? It's nestled inside Virginia's crucifix. I touch it every day as I head out the door.

LYRICS

Sharing a car with a 17-year old can be crazy making. Whenever Julie uses the car, the seat gets moved up too far, the mirror is rearranged, and the gas tank is left empty. Then there is the radio. I can't count how many times I've gotten in the car, only to be blasted by music that makes my head hurt. I mean, I listen to country music for a reason. I can understand the words. When I listen to music I hear the lyrics first, probably because words are so much a part of my life. Julie? She's a musician. She hears the instruments first, often not hearing the lyrics until they're pointed out to her.

Over the last couple of years, music has become a much more important part of my life. I can't believe how often I've encountered a song whose lyrics perfectly matched where I was in this life. When I was at my lowest, *"Bridge Over Troubled Waters"* (Simon and Garfunkel) reminded me that I was not alone. When I was wounded, *"It's a Little Too Late"* (Toby Keith), allowed me to grieve. When I felt discouraged, *"I Run for Life"* (Melissa Ethridge) gave me hope. As I began to heal from my divorce, I listened repeatedly to *"Lost Highway"* (Bon Jovi). My personal anthem has become *"It's All Good "*(Toby again). What they all have in common is a message I needed at that particular moment. I found my story in those songs and found a way to share an experience even when by myself.

Julie, on the other hand, feels the rhythm of the music. She appreciates the guitar riffs and the piano solos, and feels the emotion of the song in a physical, rather than cognitive way. For Julie, music makes her forget where she is at that moment. She is suspended in time and place and can appreciate how a guitarist or pianist interprets the song. Julie is moved by the sound, by the instruments working together. Heavy metal is not noise to her; it is collaboration. I really wish I could hear the instruments in the same way.

I don't want to dismiss something before I really give it a chance. Rarely in this life have I been open to new types of music. I actually fell asleep at a Steppenwolf concert! I mean, music of the 80's might well have never happened as often as I had the radio on! I held on to the music of my youth, never opening the door to new sounds. But the last few years have left me curious, left me wondering what I've missed. I want to listen to different kinds of music, to hear what Julie hears. She is so much more able to hear all the notes of this life and to imagine all the different ways they can be combined. What a gift.

As Julie's departure from home creeps ever closer, I'm looking for ways to have more shared experiences. Letting go means I also need to find ways to stay connected. I want to learn from her and hear the music behind the words; to experience not just the story of the song, but to feel the mood. While this opens up a whole new set of radio buttons, it pushes the borders of my comfort zone.

We are hitting the road tomorrow to re-visit the colleges on Julie's list. Up to this point, she and I have survived car trips by implementing what we have come to call the "my song-your song" rule. I listen to my station for one song, then it's her turn. On a two day road trip, this might not work as well as it does on a trip to the grocery store. I anticipate, in order to avoid the battle of the buttons, Julie will want to plug in her iPod and listen to only 'her' music. While this would solve the immediate problem, it does little to create a common experience, to bond over the music. I plan to invite myself to listen in, to let Julie control the buttons. I want to hear what she hears, to understand the pull of the notes. I want Julie to hear the stories the songs tell and I want her to teach me the stories of the instruments. Together, we can then share the experience – and the music.

GOLF

I've always been fascinated by the game of golf. I envy even the average duffer for being able to whack around a little ball with a big club. The game is as much mental as physical, and incredibly social, which is why I'm so drawn to the links. I love listening to people tell golf stories and am often amazed they can remember a particular shot on a particular hole on a course they played decades earlier! This is a game people can continue to play, regardless of age or physical fitness.

I come from a long line of fairway walkers and can't hit a golf ball to save my life. Twenty plus years ago, I took lessons, and the charming pro I consulted suggested I find something better to do with my time. I believed the jerk and never followed through on learning this beautiful game. I believed him rather than listening to my own instincts. I was reminded this week of the foolishness of that decision.

The main reason I hoped to learn the game was to play with my mother's sisters. Having lost my mother, Virginia, when I was just four years old, I always viewed these women as her voice on earth. Florence, Margaret, and Irene were all avid golfers and I've been told they played together often, well into their 70's. This sharing of time and experience had to be rich with both wisdom and laughter. In times of both joy and sorrow, golf may have been the time they could rejoice and grieve with one another, as only sisters can do.

I often thought if I could golf, I'd someday be able to play a round or two with them. I didn't get to know these women, well, as a child, but their presence in my life was strong. I felt their influence, a bit like living guardian angels. Through golfing, I thought I could share in stories of my mother. I imagined learning of her through their eyes, through their memories. I certainly could have done this off the course but saw golfing as a way to share time with my aunts as perhaps my mother might, had she not died so young. I know Florence, Irene, and Margaret would have welcomed me into the foursome with open arms and open hearts.

Sadly, it's too late. Margaret passed away a number of years ago, Irene is now in a long term care facility, and Florence passed this week. At the funeral, I watched as my cousins embraced each other as only people who know each other well can do. I listened as they shared stories of their individual families. I looked at photographs of people with whom I share blood, but little else.

As I spent time with cousins who remember me more than I remember them, I was struck by one thought. Why didn't I take the opportunity to know my aunts better; to share in the stories they could have told on or off the greens? I imagine they wanted to tell the stories as much as I wanted to hear them. More importantly, why didn't I take the opportunity to enrich my life with these incredible women who could have taught me so much about life, love, and family? I honestly don't have a good answer.

I'm more than blessed with a life full of strong females. Sisters, friends, and nieces all enrich my world on a daily basis. They have been my teachers on how to live a life of confidence. Through them I am rooted to this earth and know how to nurture those I love. Yet I can't help feeling that on a very deep level, I failed to take advantage of relationships that might have enriched my ancestral connections, enriched my knowledge of who I am.

Fortunately, it's not too late. I don't need to make the same mistake twice. I'm a part of the current generation of beautiful Cassidy women. I no longer need the stories of my mother as much as I want to be part of the legacy created by her sisters. I want to share in the creation of new stories and new memories. I may not be able to catch up, but I can certainly keep pace.

As I grieved the loss of Florence, I exchanged e-mail addresses with each of my cousins. I vowed to stay in better touch; to learn more about their lives, their families and our ancestors. I vowed that it would not take another funeral to bring us together. Even though I don't know if my cousins golf, I plan to find out and at least drive the cart.

BAND-AIDS

Every month when I have my eyebrows waxed, I complain to my stylist, Midge, that it hurts. She insists on ripping off the sticky strip quickly and even though I know it is coming, I'm always surprised by how much I'm jarred. Each time I tell her to be kind, then tense up when I think she is ready to yank. Each month she tells me to shut up. I'm convinced Midge tricks me into thinking I will feel no pain, and then, bam! I'm convinced she enjoys it, and I am equally convinced that there has to be a less painful way to remove that pesky hair.

You see, I'm a rip-the-band-aid-off-slowly kind of gal. A one-toe-in-the-water gal. I like my discomfort in small doses. At the pool or beach, I sit on the side until my legs are adjusted to the water temperature. Next, I go in up to my waist. Then I swim. My sister, Barbie, jumps right in and is underwater before my ankles are wet. When riding my bike and approaching a hill, I like to pause at the bottom, brace myself, then get ready for the climb. My riding partners take the "object in motion stays in motion" approach. Naturally, I'm always the last one to the top. I'm convinced that if I ease into the pain, it won't hurt as much. That philosophy is not proving to be true when it comes to Julie leaving home.

Julie is visiting her father, who lives in the Virgin Islands, and I thought it'd be good practice for when she leaves for college. Normally when she's gone, I look forward to the time alone. I can come and go as I please, have anyone over that I want, and stay out late. I'm not negotiating the use of the car nor sharing the bathroom. The house looks exactly the same when I get home as it did when I left. I love that freedom for a few days or even a week. Then I begin to miss her and to feel restless. This time I started to miss her as soon as I dropped her off at the airport. This time I knew that even though she will be back in eight days, all too soon it will be a month. Then two. Then maybe more. That perceived freedom starts to look an awful lot like loneliness. This rite of passage, as normal as it is, has me wondering how to manage the shift. Millions of parents go through it every day and survive. These feelings are certainly not unique to me, just new.

I've defined myself as a mother for 18 years and, although I know that I will always be Julie's mom, that role is shifting fast. As it should. The problem is really not Julie leaving home, the problem is in having defined myself as a one dimensional person, as defining myself ONLY as a mother. I know I'm much more. I am a counselor, a sister, a friend, a biker, and (gasp) a writer! The more I settle into these roles, the more whole I become and less vulnerable when there is a change.

Is it going to hurt when Julie leaves for college? Yes. Like hell. I can't prevent that pain no matter how much I prepare. I need to reflect that Julie moving on is just one more indicator that I have done my job well; that she is ready to leave means she is ready to take on new roles, and that's a good thing. She will come home, even this week, with lots of stories to share. I can't wait to hear them and be able to share mine. After all, with six whole days of freedom left, who knows what could happen?

STUFF

Julie's trophy collection does not include one trophy that has her name on it. Oh, she has her fair share of ribbons and varsity letters earned over the years, but her trophy collection is made up of statuettes with someone else's moniker on them. It started when she was seven and spotted the "golden woman" (a bowling trophy) that sat atop a pile of "free stuff" on a neighbor's lawn. Never one to let something valuable get thrown away, Julie begged to save the woman from certain death. Like any normal mom who thinks there is already too much junk in the house, I refused. I continued to ignore her pleas until my favorite junk collecting friend suggested I was being a bit rigid and that I should just let her have the damn thing! He assured me that in a week's time, Julie would lose interest and move on to a new treasure. I found myself sneaking across the street to retrieve the doomed dame and clean her up. I can still feel Julie's young arms being thrown around my waist when she came home from school to find the stupid thing on her bed. In the ten years since, that trophy has never left her room and has been joined by a few more given to her by the same junk collecting friend.

My friend, Patty, is moving in two short weeks. She is joyously downsizing from a 3- bedroom colonial with tons of yard work, to a 2-bedroom apartment with a balcony perfect for container gardening. At first, the idea of packing everything was daunting but now she is quite happy to be throwing or giving away things that for years she felt she needed. Julie is just beginning to define her life by her stuff, while Patty is realizing that her life is defined by relationships and experiences, not by her possessions. I am somewhere in between on that continuum.

As I look around my home, I realize that I have more vases than I will ever have flowers, more dishes than guests. There are far too many possessions that I hang onto "just in case". I cherish the things that belonged to my mother, grandmother, and aunts. I find comfort in family photographs and I'm nurtured by those reminders of moments shared with all the people who have graced my life. I like spending time in a place that feels comfortable, and I've worked hard to create a space with things that make people feel welcome.

I began to reflect on which of my many treasures I could live without. The reality is that I could live without all of it. Most of us have far more than we need and we hold on to stuff because of what it represents, rather than its usefulness. I haven't used my mother's china in a couple of years, but every time I open that cupboard I'm reminded of my family history and the many meals shared on those plates. My hand-made quilts are packed away, but when I see them I'm reminded of the quiet moments when I stitched those tiny pieces together. Tucked inside the crucifix is the penny I'm sure my mother sent from heaven. The fact is, I'm not ready to part with any of these possessions. My "stuff" is a life scrapbook and a record of my travels. The value is defined and understood only by me and I will ultimately decide when it's no longer needed. I should remember the same is true whenever I am tempted to do a clean sweep of Julie's room.

If I needed to start over with only one of my many spoils which would I choose? I'm not talking about what I would need for survival, but something to serve as a compass for the future. Would I take the china or a photograph? Would I want that 1960 penny or the rosary Julie brought me from New York? What about Julie's first piece of art from Kindergarten? Perhaps I would take my bike, which keeps me moving forward, or my father's watch, which grounds me to my past. All good choices. The problem is, I'm a master at knowing what other people need, lousy at knowing what I don't.

At a very tender age, Julie was instinctively drawn to those things that other people were discarding. I've been told it is a common adoption issue. Maybe so, because over the years, that first trophy has come to symbolize Julie's core belief that everyone has value. To this day, it holds a place of honor in her room and represents a tender moment between the two of us. So I think, with Julie's permission, I would start over with the trophy of the golden woman. She really is quite beautiful.

WEEDS

Every spring I like to fancy myself a gardener. The idea of nurturing small plants into beautiful flowers is quite appealing. I envision all the blooming colors gracing my yard and eventually my kitchen table. I imagine strolling the grounds early in the morning, sipping my tea, beginning my day full of beauty and serenity. I run into a snag each year as I have great difficulty figuring out which green things are flowers, and which are weeds, as they all look the same to me. This problem has destroyed more than one garden.

Many years ago, with my first home, I inherited a beautiful perennial bed. I couldn't believe the array of flowers: tulips, irises, roses, lilies, daisies, all arranged in perfect groups of height and color. I was eager to keep the garden in the same splendor I had found it and was ready to rid it of anything that interfered with its growth. I began to pull on the long spindly stalks that seemed to be choking the flowers. They were everywhere and had to be contained! Once I had a large pile of the prickly stuff, I proudly sat back to admire my work. My husband took one look at the weeds and quickly pointed out that I had just cleared the garden of all the poppies. For the five years we lived in that house, never once did another poppy bloom. I did leave some really tall onion shoots because I was convinced the little bulb on top would produce a lovely flower. In our next house, I stuck with marigolds and impatiens.

Another move came with another large perennial plot. This one was planted over the property line and shared with the older woman who lived next door. For 20 years, Mrs. Cook had worked the garden with the woman from whom we bought the house. Again, the flowers were spectacular and I worried about caring for my half. Mrs. Cook was in the yard every morning pinching, grooming, and weeding. She watered and fed the plants and moved them around to keep them from getting too crowded. Her daily attention kept the garden lush and thriving. It was then that I began to learn that tending a garden is a lot like tending a relationship: you have to recognize and remove the weeds and nurture the new growth.

Every day brings the commitment of caring for my existing relationships and the prospect of new ones. My "perennial" relationships are healthy and can survive the occasional drought or lack of attention. My closest relationships are strong because they have been nurtured consistently over time and their roots are established. They can stand on their own and do not need daily attention. I have a dear friend I have not seen in four years, but when we talk every few weeks, it's as if the conversation was never interrupted. She knows my soul.

It can be difficult to recognize those things that limit a new relationship. In my attempts to introduce a new variety to my garden, I worry I will find myself bereft of color if I weed people out, even if they limit my own growth. I have to fight the tendency to change who I am to meet the expectations of someone else. I'm always surprised when I find myself feeling this way, because the most beautiful gardens are those filled with lots of different kinds of flowers. They complement each other rather than compete.

As Julie's graduation looms ever closer, I fear if I don't add new relationships now I will be lonely. I worry I will spend too much time on Saturday nights with the dog, and I will be forgotten. Yes, these thoughts are irrational, but fears at 3 a.m. rarely make sense. Even though my relationship garden is pretty full, I do sometimes feel alone. Not lonely, just alone. I wonder if I will fail to recognize when an opportunity is right in front of me. In those moments I remember the poppies and feel just a tad bit scared that I will once again not recognize the beauty that lies among the thorns.

I want to plant new seeds and see what comes up, to blend new growth with my perennials. Mrs. Cook taught me that plants can always be moved around to make room for more. She taught me the best gardens are the ones that get both sun and rain, and she taught me that the best gardeners are patient.

BRIDGES

I'm a girl. I don't know or care what a piston is. I don't know how to change a tire and when something breaks, the best thing I can do is make a phone call. When I have participated in general trivia contests, I defer to my smarter friends, or I cheat. I certainly do not have enough science smarts to understand how bridges get built. To me, they are an engineering marvel and can be breathtaking as they arch across a body of water or valley. Although not as complicated in their design, covered bridges are striking in their simplicity and serenity. Funny thing, I am actually pretty afraid of these engineering marvels.

Let me clarify; this fear has never kept me from crossing any platforms and small ones don't cause tremendous anxiety. When I am traveling across a very large span, (think the Golden Gate), I have flashes of the whole thing collapsing and of trying to get out of a sinking car. When I do have to cross a bridge, I want assurance that the structure is secure, no cracks or loose bolts, and trust it's strong enough to support the weight. Even then, I often open the car windows when crossing so as to allow myself an escape hatch.

When Julie and I did our recent college road trip, I shared my worries with her. She, of course, had a grand time making fun of me as we crossed over the Niagara River, and felt the need to remind me each time we crossed even a small stretch of metal. Even though she was teasing me, we did have some interesting conversation about fears and worries and how they get developed. Where did this fear come from and what exactly do bridges represent?

It got me thinking about whether our lives are a series of bridges. Each event or challenge moves us across the arches of our lives until we arrive on the other side. If this is true, then I am smack dab in the middle, where my anxiety is always the greatest. Because during bridge-crossing, my fear takes over at the peak, then dissipates as I begin the downward approach to the shore. This could mean the second half of my life is going to be easier than the first. Not a bad thought. It seems the climb is always tougher than the descent.

Instead though, I believe life is a series of crossings. Sometimes we may be on a draw-bridge which opens up, forcing us to slow down and take stock; slow down and wait for the trouble to pass.

At other times it may seem like we are on a simple rope trestle, hundreds of feet above the forest floor. In those moments, we need to rely on our gut instinct, put one foot in front of the other and keep our eyes focused in front of us. When we make it across, we immediately kiss the ground, and remember our success was in our ability to keep our footing. Balance is indeed the reason that bridges rarely collapse beneath us.

To me, any one of these arches represents how we stay linked to people, to places, and to events. Both on the path to a destination and the road back, the bridges represent the promise of a new opportunity and a reminder from where we came. Their strength comes not from the concrete and braces, but from the people who have crossed before and are waiting.

I'm still not sure what keeps bridges from collapsing under the weight of the traffic. But I am sure that my life is kept together by the people on the bridge with me. The people who love me are the open window; they are what keeps the troubles of this life from being overwhelming and they provide me with the safety net I need. Because of them I'm confident of making it safely to the other side.

It took a few hours, but eventually Julie lost interest in teasing me about my fear. When we had to re-cross the mighty Niagara and the traffic slowed down, she actually checked in to see if I was okay. Moving slowly across this huge mass of metal and bolts made me sweat a bit but it was good to know that the person traveling along side was willing to hold me up.

TICKET

My love affair with movie theaters began in second grade when Mom and Dad (he remarried 2 years after my mother's death), took me downtown to see Cary Grant in "Father Goose". The theater was majestic and magical and I couldn't wait to go back again and again. In high school, I was lucky enough to land the job of candy girl at the mall multiplex, so I had special privileges; I could see any movie, at any theater in town, for free. All I had to do was call my manager who would arrange for tickets to be waiting for me. Very little time went by without taking in a movie at either my theater or the competition's. I went to see comedies, dramas, horror films, and even a few that were sub-titled. I saw a lot of movies in those years and because I could always take a friend, I had a lot of movie dates.

After a few months of pushing milk-duds and popcorn, I was promoted to ticket sales and could see who arrived with whom. I saw families with young children, nervous first dates, and older couples holding hands. Groups of teenagers and middle-aged women would come after shopping at the mall. For the most part, they were anonymous strangers who smiled and bought a ticket. But I always noticed when someone came in solo. Their smile, in the mind of a 17-year old, seemed just a bit forced. I could imagine nothing worse than having to go to the movies alone. I couldn't fathom anyone would want to sit through a movie by themselves. I mean, how pitiful must their life be if they couldn't find SOMEONE to bring along? I promised myself that I would never be caught eating my Twizzlers alone.

I kept that promise for 35 years. In college I could always find someone to take to a movie. Almost all my first dates involved dinner and the movies and I married a man who shared my passion for the cinema. Although I could no longer score free tickets, we went to the movies a lot. It was our favorite date night and we were willing to pay a babysitter big bucks to indulge in our favorite shared past-time. When the marriage fell apart after 25 years, I suddenly found myself without a movie date. Sadly there was not a group of friends who wanted to spend time with a newly divorced woman. My married friends didn't know what to do with me, and I hadn't nurtured many relationships separate from my marriage.

At first, I compensated by dragging my pre-teen daughter

whenever she wasn't too embarrassed to be seen with me. Then I began to invite my adult nieces, who just felt sorry for me. I signed up for HBO and learned how to work the VCR so I could just rent whatever movie I wanted to see. But I ultimately missed the sights and smells of a movie house. I missed the cup holders and comfortable seats. I missed the trailers of coming attractions and I missed being surrounded by the darkness. But mostly I really missed the disgustingly good, bad-for-your -heart, popcorn. There is not a microwave in the world that can duplicate the real thing. So I finally had to acknowledge that I was one of those pitiful people who would have to stand in front of the ticket girl and buy a ticket for one. I was terrified. I made a plan.

First, I had to choose the right theater. I didn't want to go to one of the old stand-alone theaters because I feared I would be one of only 11 people there and more conspicuous. I didn't want to head to Cinema City with 20 screens because I worried about the number of couples I would see. I decided to head to the smaller six-screen movie theater that had, ironically, been built to replace the very one where I worked in high school. It was close to home and, even though I knew I might see a lot of familiar faces, it felt the most comfortable. Next came selecting the best day, time and movie.

My favorite time to go to the movies is on a Saturday night. Since I associate movie night with date night, I decided that for my first time going solo I would stick to a 5:00 Saturday showing. Then I chose a serious drama over a romantic comedy; I wanted to be able to walk out alone in thoughtful silence, rather than listening to the shared laughter among friends and lovers. I knew I would miss the post-movie conversation that always takes place on the car ride home, but at least everyone would be more reflective as they headed to the exit. When I opened the paper to the entertainment section, the movie title practically leapt off the page: "Doubt". Now all that was left was actually going. I parked the car, took a deep breath and figured that there were three things standing between me and the start of that movie: buying the ticket, getting the popcorn and choosing my seat.

I approached the ticket booth with trepidation, hoping that whoever was selling tickets would think I was meeting someone inside and not really the pitiful figure I remembered from my youth. I looked at the young girl selling tickets and flashed back to my own years behind the counter. I looked her in the eye, almost daring her to challenge my request for one ticket. Barely looking at me, she slid the ticket under the plastic divider and told me to enjoy the show. I smiled, casually took the ticket and headed to the entrance where the guy taking the ticket was much more interested in the two 20-year old young things behind me. Again, no one really noticed I was alone.

Next came the concession stand. Since it's not unusual for one person to stand in line while their partner looks for the best seats, I didn't stand out. I quietly stood in line and indulged myself with both popcorn and candy. Forget all the lectures about emotional eating, this was completely necessary! Armed with my snacks and a super soda, I headed into the theater where I had already decided to sit in the back row. I usually like to sit in the middle, but this was my virgin voyage and I wanted to take it slowly. I found a spot on the aisle and began to settle in. As the seats began to fill up and the lights were dimmed, I noticed that no one was staring and pointing at the poor lonely woman sitting by herself. They were looking at the screen.

I waited for the show to begin, thinking of the benefits of going solo: no one was going to lean over and tell me what they thought was going to happen—I was not going to have to wrangle for the arm rest—no one was going to sip off of my soda or eat my popcorn. I was free to enjoy the movie on my terms. Enjoy it I did! I watched Meryl Streep, knowing she would once again score an Oscar nomination. I also knew I had scored major points in accepting my life as a single woman. I could feel my own self-doubts fading with the ending credits.

When I left the theater, I found myself looking at the people around me. Yes, people were chatting, but I also noticed the number of people with dates or friends who were not talking to each other at all. I realized that was me not too long ago. I suddenly began to wonder how many movies I had seen during my marriage when I *really* was very much alone. I wondered if we spent so much time going to the movies because we had stopped finding things to talk about. On this victorious night, I did not feel alone. I was reunited with that young candy girl working her first real job. I became re-acquainted with the college student who left home for the first time. I was joined by the young woman who put herself through grad school. I was bolstered by the woman now raising a daughter on her own. I was in pretty fine company.

I climbed into the car and felt a bit of excitement about my accomplishment. For 35 years I had believed that lone movie-goers were lost souls who had no one to spend time with. We aren't lost. We know exactly where we're headed. We are simply living the stories of our lives with a script that is not yet finished.

WARNINGS

One of my favorite TV shows as a kid was "Lost in Space". I loved the idea of the whole family traveling together to a strange and distant planet. Their journey started as an adventure but ended up being a fight for survival. My favorite character was the robot, who regularly issued warnings of impending trouble: "Danger, Will Robinson! Danger!" For the last two weeks, I have felt like Captain Robinson and have taken heed of warnings that keep popping up. There is, indeed, something lurking in the shadows of my heart and to ignore the emotional alerts could mean trouble.

The warnings began a few weeks back when Julie made her final decision about which college to attend. The choice had been narrowed down to two: the small private liberal arts school and the large public institution. Her COLLEGE COUNSELOR MOTHER recommended the more intimate, protective environment, but no, she went for the school where she felt the most comfortable; the one where she felt she'd be the most successful. Julie selected the large school based on her instincts, her needs, and her dreams. I felt a very subtle shift in the ground under my feet; Julie decided what was best for her. Warning #1.

Then it was time for the annual Spirit Day at school. The day consists of competitions between the class levels and involves 600 girls screaming for six hours. The pandemonium of their activity is equivalent to that of an earthquake! As they have for the past four years, friends crowded into Julie's room the previous night to get ready. I got little sleep as I listened to them practicing the class cheer and coordinating the blue outfits and make-up that would identify them as seniors. The joy was palpable in the sound of their laughter. After a healthy breakfast of donuts and coffee, they all piled into my car, singing and ready to show the school who was in charge. This would be their last spirit day; their last chance to demonstrate their class unity, the last time I would witness Julie screaming with her classmates. Again I felt the ground shift ever so slightly. Warning #2.

An hour later, during the singing of the alma mater, I caught sight of Julie in the sea of blue faces, belting out the song with a huge smile. This time the shift was more pronounced and I had to fight back tears. Julie is soon to become someone who looks back on her high school days instead of someone who navigates the familiar hallways of the building. My work day will no longer include having her stop in my office for a chat, an Advil, or money! The subtle rumbling was getting louder. Warning #3.

A week later, the deadline arrived for ordering the yearbook. Parents of seniors can purchase an ad congratulating their daughter on graduation. Julie's father, my former husband, now lives out of town and I had to negotiate the plan over the phone. He insisted on a full page ad which meant I had to, on my own, dig through 17 years of pictures to find the ones that would show all her light and beauty. Sorting through box after box of Julie's childhood, my brain was filled with images of her as a baby, a toddler, and a 10-year old. I recalled vacations at the beach, getting braces, and trips to the ER for the occasional stitch. I remembered her tears over fights with friends and over our divorce. That night, I dreamt of Julie and Woody, the dog who was her constant companion for 15 years. When I awoke, I almost wished the earth would open up and swallow the ache in my heart. Warning #4.

The ongoing question remains: what happens when I'm not there to witness and experience her daily triumphs and struggles? What happens when I'm no longer falling asleep on the couch waiting for her to come home at night? What happens when I feel like the ground *is* split wide open beneath me?

What happens is that the earth *will* settle. It won't return to the exact same place and it will look different. The landscape may change but the background will remain the same. Yes, the earth will indeed settle and I will, at some point, feel the ground is again stable. I'll regain my balance, and I might even feel like dancing.

Despite these warnings, the rumblings in the earth are happy shifts. They are reminders that Julie is healthy and happy, and that the ground beneath her is solid. She can handle more than I give her credit for. She can't sew on a button, but she can navigate airports, job interviews, and housing registration forms. Julie is ready.

The next few weeks are going to include a number of mini-earthquakes and even some aftershocks. Julie is going to have her own emotional moments as she brings this part of her life to a close. Senior class picture was today. Prom is in 10 days. Graduation in just 37. "Danger, Will Robinson! Danger!"

BRICKS

As a kid, I loved the story, *The Three Little Pigs*. I remember thinking that the first two pigs were silly creatures who didn't understand the need for safety. The third little guy was the wise pig who looked at the failures of the other pigs and made a structure that would eventually defeat the big bad wolf. When I'm walking the neighborhood, I find myself drawn to brick houses. To me they represent strength, stability, and protection. They are not easily weathered and can resist the effects of storms better than houses made of wood. In my own little brick house, I rarely hear a storm raging just outside, and I feel protected by a silent force that is standing behind me. For that reason, brick houses make me think of my dad.

Dad is not an expressive, touchy-feely kind of guy. He is creative, a problem-solver, and has a great sense of humor. My dad is pragmatic to a fault and has always taken the approach that when faced with one of life's storms, you "just go about your business." He's always seen me as too emotional, but in times of crisis he always has my back. As my father, he has served as the foundation of my ability to move on. We disagree politically but, strangely enough, Dad is one of the most tolerant people I know. I've inherited his droopy eyelids, his stubbornness, and his love of comfort food. It was he who found me the best gift ever: my daughter.

Dad knew how much I wanted to share my love with a child, and it was he who introduced me to Julie's birthparents when he learned of their need to place their daughter for adoption. He was the first person in my family to lay eyes on Julie. It was my unemotional dad who phoned me crying, to tell me if I could be in South Dakota the next day, then I could be a mother. It was the moment in my life I felt the most loved.

Julie has grown into a beautiful young woman and her grandfather has never stopped asking how "the baby is". He finds it hard to believe that she is actually headed to college and he delights in her accomplishments. My dad is proud of all of his grandkids and relishes any time he can spend with them; they are his on-going legacy. So it has been hard for everyone to see this man, one of the bricks of my life, weather the storm of Parkinson's Disease. For the past six years, this illness has continued to chip away at his mobility and his independence, but not at his spirit.

This man refuses to give in to the punishment his body takes on a daily basis. His will is as strong as ever and he never stops trying to fight the effects of this disease. I wonder sometimes how much more he can take. Oh, he occasionally feels sorry for himself and feels discouraged and betrayed by his body, but then he goes golfing. Literally, he goes golfing! Strapping himself into a specially converted golf cart, Dad can drive to the ball, rotate his seat, and stand to take a swing. The way he plays the game has changed, but his sense of competition remains the same. Like a brick house, Dad's body seems able to sustain the storm that continues to rage on. I so respect his commitment to not let this disease get the better of his soul. He's taught me perseverance and determination, two traits that I hope I've passed on to Julie.

Like this brick house I call home, my dad is the silent force that provides shelter. Brick by brick he built a family that does stand strong and stands up for each other. We are all fiercely independent, strong individuals who have learned from him that when we feel sorry for ourselves, our task is to get up each morning and start again. I don't think he ever spoke those actual words. He just lives them. Every day.

When Julie graduates in a few short weeks, I pray Dad can be there to share in her success. He's responsible for bringing Julie into this family and I know they both want to share the moment. Unfortunately, each day brings a new challenge and he may physically not be able to negotiate the event. I hope he knows that even though he and Julie do not share DNA, she will carry him in her heart as she accepts her diploma.

Dad has protected me from the big bad wolf for over 50 years. Perhaps it's my turn to return the favor and provide him with a bit of shelter from the storm. I can't slow the progress of his disease, make it go away. I can spend time with him in a way that distracts from the blowing winds. I guess I better go buy some bricks.

SUMMERTIME

We all have memories of summers we thought would never end; no school, no structure, no responsibilities beyond helping with the dishes and keeping our rooms clean. The days stretched out in front of us with endless possibilities. Being bored was never an option because to admit having nothing to do meant your mother could find plenty for you to do. So you hit the bricks after breakfast, came home for lunch and dinner and spent the time in between bike riding, swimming, playing kick ball and, on really hot days, popping tar bubbles. Sometimes you just sat with your friends on the lawn plucking dandelion stems. There were no structured activities beyond going from house to house to see who could play, and whose mother might let kids in the house. You were rich if you earned a buck selling lemonade, and bedtime came only after the whole neighborhood had played kick the can in the dark. Lucky was the kid who was allowed to set up the sprinkler in their yard or who got a slip-n-slide. Summer meant freedom, fun, and fireworks. It meant getting a tan just from being outside, young. It meant being alive.

Julie's graduation creeps ever closer and to avoid looking at the emotional hail storm due to hit over the next few weeks, I started to think about what I could do this summer to challenge my body and soul. A friend and I listed all the things we want to try over the warm months: she came up with paintball; I came up with riding a roller coaster (one of the really big ones), kayaking, going to the horse races, and golf. Add in that I plan to complete a 100 mile bike ride and you have a pretty full three months. When I shared the list with a nephew, he suggested I was having one hell of a mid-life crisis!

In my head that creates visions of sports cars, plastic surgery, and cabana boys. Since I can't afford any of those, my mid-life crisis is all about challenging my "I'm too old" thinking. Sometimes I think I got old before I finished being young. I mean, the roller coaster thing should've been out of my system decades ago. In my 30's, I was all about settling down, being responsible and practical. My idea of risk was venturing into shallow ocean water during jelly fish alerts! I wrote a will and decided I needed to be a grownup; to role model appropriate behavior for Julie. Fortunately I never limited her sense of adventure while I was putting an end to mine.

As an adult, my general reaction to trying something new is skepticism; I too often dismiss an idea before I really consider the possibilities. I quickly find a reason not to do something or decide it's unsafe. I tell myself that at my age I don't need to feel excited, I don't need to be thrilled. I don't ride the Millennium Roller Coaster because I might pass out, feel squeamish or fall off! What bull. I don't ride because I feel scared: scared of new experiences and scared of new feelings.

My whole professional life as a counselor has been about exploring other peoples' feelings, of helping others examine their emotions and choices. It's then somewhat surprising that I'm an expert at denying my own. I'm really good at pretending I'm fulfilled. To acknowledge that I am out of touch with my own feelings and actually limiting my own personal growth is a bit uncomfortable. It's much easier to find excuses and to place the blame on others. But I really have no one else to blame. I can't blame my childhood. I can't blame my marriage. I can't blame parenthood. I have to look only to myself for the reasons that I don't pursue adventures that may make me feel more alive. It's time to find a better balance between taking care of this life and caring to have a better one.

Here I sit, at the half way point of my life. OK, maybe a bit further along than that but with plenty of years and energy left. Last summer I went white water rafting and zip-lining. Even though paint ball is not at the top of my list, why NOT do it? The kayaking is set for late June; the horse races for July. A two day bike ride for charity is in August and will be the warm-up for the 100 miler in September. Golf will take most of the summer just to get off the first tee! It feels again as if the summer and my life are full of endless possibilities. No, this isn't a mid-life crisis. It's a mid-life awakening. A chance to take risks, have fun, and maybe rediscover the joy of feeling this life. A chance to re-awaken my spirit.

Julie asked me to ride the Millennium on her birthday in June. She wants to sit in the front car. While the view from that spot will scare the hell out of me, the view if I stay on the ground is terrifying. It's the perfect way to kick off another summer of my second youth.

31

GRASS

When my older brother, Bob, left home for college it was quite traumatic. I was very worried about what life was going to be like without him around. I was worried because Bob was the one who cut the grass and someone else was going to get that job. I hoped it wouldn't be me. My dad decided to have "tryouts." First he had my younger sister, Barbie, cut a few rows. She didn't do a very good job, making the rows crooked, and missing huge patches of grass in between. My dad patted her on the back, shook his head a bit, and motioned that it was my turn. Since it had worked pretty well for Barbie, and Dad hadn't gotten that mad, I duplicated her efforts. I waited for the similar pat on the back, the sad shake of the head, but instead was told to "knock it off and finish cutting the grass". Despite my best attempts to lose, I had won the job. Thus began my love-hate relationship with yard work.

I despised cutting my parent's lawn. It was huge, hilly, and always too hot. It took a good two hours to cut the whole thing and I couldn't believe I would just have to do it all over again in a week! But I loved the orderliness of the job and how neat the rows looked when I was finished. I loved the smell; Lord how I loved the intoxicating smell.

I spent four years vowing to myself that when I moved out, I would never again cut grass. Between apartment living and later marrying a man obsessed with yard work, I was able to keep that promise for over 30 years. Then I moved into this little house with a big yard. By default, I once again won the job of lawn care provider. Last summer, I tried to find anyone and everyone to do the work. I paid nephews, Julie's friends and once even hired the guy mowing my neighbor's lawn just to get it done. I remembered what I hated about the job and complained bitterly. When no one else was available, I bit the bullet and fired up the mower.

As this lawn care season arrived, I decided to remember what I did like about the job and welcomed the task. Even though mowing is a repetitive, thankless job, I realize there is something I love about it: everyone leaves me alone. For that hour, I can be completely alone with my thoughts. I can think, plan, day-dream, and enjoy my own company. Believe it or not, I have begun to look forward to that hour. What I like most about this time of my week is the lack of expectations: I don't have to talk, I don't have to

32

listen, and I can look like crap because I am, after all, doing yard work. Sometimes I mow from left to right, sometimes from top to bottom, and sometimes in continuous squares that get smaller and smaller. I can start in the front or the back, and I can breathe deeply the rich scent of summer.

I realized, while doing the mundane task of cutting grass, that I'm beginning to embrace the one thing I'm most afraid of…being alone. Choosing to find time to just be with myself makes me better at being with others. Having my own experiences to share makes sharing time with friends richer. I don't want company for everything I do and I don't want to be in constant communication with everyone I know. I refuse to "plug in" when I am walking or biking because I want to take in the natural life sounds. I may seek company when there is no one around, but I also sometimes want to be alone when people are knocking on the door.

Julie leaving for college in August is not what I have to be afraid of. Being alone is not what I should fear. What I need to fear is expecting other people to fulfill me. There's not another soul on this earth who can meet all of my needs, and I can't imagine that I'm all someone else needs. In any relationship, people need to know the line between intimacy and space and allow room for each to be nurtured. I don't fear growing old alone as much as I fear not always learning something new about the people I love and constantly surprising those who may love me. If every moment is shared, if every thought is spoken, then what is left to discover? I've made that mistake. I won't again.

If you happen to see me pushing the mower back and forth, smile and know that I really am enjoying myself and the gift of time alone. But I could really use some help with trimming the hedges.

BOOKSHELF

My favorite movie scene of all time is in Disney's "Beauty and the Beast". I remember taking Julie to see the film and sucking in my breath when the Beast presents Belle with the gift of the library. As he opens the door to expose the walls lined with volumes and volumes of books, I felt I finally had the image for my life story. You see, I've long used a bookshelf to describe my life and here was the exact vision I had imagined: a room filled with books from ceiling to floor. A room filled with the stories of this life.

In my personal life library, the bookshelves hold every story of my life, both good and bad. The most accessible row has plenty of room for novels currently being written. As time passes books get moved up and over so that there's room for new offerings. Each one stays in the collection so they can be re-read as needed. I can take down the needed volume, remember the event, and then gently put the book back in its proper place. I can retrieve any story (happy or sad) at any time, and keep it down until I'm ready to put it back. In writing these essays of becoming an empty nester, I have found myself spending a lot of time in my library. Each new feeling is being viewed through the lens of a previous one and memories are floating in and out of conscious thought.

Every May, I pull down the bound pages that tell the story of my mother, Virginia, who died when she was 29. This week marked 50 years since she lost her battle with breast cancer. My life has been significantly defined by this loss and it's been at the core of how I approach my life, my parenting, and my relationships. It has defined who I am as a woman, a mother, a wife, and a friend. It is at the center of my emotional strength.

I might feel hesitant about taking on physical challenges (although that is changing), but rarely have I backed away from an emotional one. I learned early that life gives us stories that we might not want to read and no one gets through this world without one or two tragedies. Oh sure, like a lot of folks, I like to visit that dark place called self-pity, but ultimately, I find a way to the light! When I do, I'm generally able to have great clarity about how to move forward and finish the chapter. I can feel sorry for myself in losing my mother so young, but it actually taught me how to handle the inevitable bumps in the road.

One of the consequences of having a parent die is the

tendency to fantasize that they were perfect. Of course I want to live up to that standard. Being an adoptive mom makes it worse, as I feel a greater responsibility to do everything right. The result is that sometimes I hold on too tight and expect too much of myself and Julie. I've held her to a higher standard and I fear that I've not always let her be her own person. I often feel judged by both her successes and failures. Many of the books on my shelf have to do with her life. As we both take this next step into our individual futures, I need to release each of us from those unrealistic expectations and begin to separate our stories.

Since day one, Julie has been collecting her own life stories and has her own bookshelf. The story of her adoption started out as mine, but really belongs to her. Starting over after the divorce is one book with separate chapters. She must decide how all the pieces fit together and she must decide if it's happy or sad. I only share my narratives with people who have been issued a library card, and so too will Julie decide with whom she shares her stories. Right now, during this crazy time, we are sharing a chapter that will mean very different things to each of us. My view of this time is colored by my history and is filled with anxiety about letting go and losing my place in her life. Her view is more likely excitement about moving on, and I have to be careful that my story doesn't take up too much space on her shelf.

This week, as my sister and I placed our annual bouquet of roses on our mother's grave, I once again turned the pages of that story. As we do every year, we marveled at the peacefulness of her resting place and wondered out loud what our life would have been like had she not died. But we drove away, ate at Arby's, and picked up the current chapter of our lives. We placed the book of our mother back on the top shelf until next year, when we will once again pull it down for a brief time. Virginia's story lives on through us and we honor her best when we do so without sadness and pain.

MOLES

I love a good carnival. I love the expressions of both anticipation and fear, the sounds of laughter combined with screaming, and of course the smells of disgustingly good fair food. My all-time favorite carnival game is "Whack a Mole". You've probably played it; the one where little mole heads keep popping up and you get to whack them with a rubber mallet. It's a great image for those times when you feel life is coming at you from all sides and you can't dodge the hammer blows. Such was my week as Julie's graduation arrived.

The first rodent came in the way of a friend in distress. I had to sit and watch a train bearing down with no ability to pull her out of the way. She is unfairly being held responsible for events out of her control, and her professional reputation is at risk. Personally, she is crushed and as the train approaches, the impending crash is painful for all who love her. I can only hold her hand and remind her, other friends and I will be here in the wake of the wreckage. It's one of those times that, having hope takes a tremendous amount of faith. We need to remember our lives are not a straight path, and sometimes our journey requires detours to places and events we didn't plan to visit.

The next critter that popped up was the impending arrival of Julie's dad. While the emotional scars from the divorce are healing, he and I are still finding our way on this path to a truce. I've worked hard to make sure Julie never feels that she has to choose one of us over the other, and her graduation is the opportunity to celebrate together the accomplishments of *our* daughter. Still, the anxiety started to build as I reflected on our history and struggled with how to share this time.

Then came the news that my parents wouldn't be able to attend Julie's graduation ceremony because it was just going to be too much of a physical challenge for Dad. Even though I had anticipated the call, I still felt tremendous sadness. The emotion wasn't because my folks were not going to watch Julie get her diploma, but rather it was because my dad wasn't *able* to attend. It was another reminder of the betrayal of his body and his struggle with the constant limitations of his illness.

Graduation day dawned with a subtle weariness. It felt like the moles were everywhere and alone I couldn't get to them all. I spent a few hours feeling sorry for myself during which time I cried a thousand tears and did enough emotional eating to destroy a week of working out. But then I decided to put on my big girl pants and face the day. Hopping on my bike, I took off for a solo ride to clear my head. It seemed to me that an unusual number of chipmunks darted away as I sped down the bike path, but perhaps that was only my imagination.

I returned home remembering that this day belonged to Julie and there was no room for my baggage. She and I spent the next few hours getting ready, ironing her graduation gown, doing our hair and just feeling the excitement of the moment. I took a million pictures in the front yard and allowed myself to feel the maternal pride that was busting through. As we pulled out of the driveway, I swear I saw a lone chipmunk peek his head out of my flower bed.

Working at the same school Julie attended, I have sat through seven previous graduations, and I was a bit worried I might not find this one memorable. I was grateful that as a faculty member I'd be able to sit in the front row and be only three feet from Julie when she received her diploma. From that vantage point I could see it all. I was part of the honor guard that our graduates walk through, each carrying a dozen red roses. I saw Julie confident, strong, and bearing little resemblance to the nervous 5-year old I dropped off at kindergarten. I could see my friend, the one staring down that train, hand Julie her diploma. I could see Julie's father proudly taking pictures of the young woman that together we brought to this moment. I could feel the gentle touch on my arm from two dear friends as they sat on either side silently supporting me as the tears again began to form. They reminded me that family is indeed a broad term and I knew that my family was both all around me and in my heart. Yes, this one was memorable because this one was personal. I could see my past, I could feel the present, and I could look forward to whatever tomorrow brings. Julie and I both graduated as we closed a chapter on one part of our lives and began taking the first few steps towards the future.

Next week is Julie's 18th birthday. It's the day, at her request, that I ride that huge roller coaster. She's upped the ante to include her desire that I sit in the front car. Now that, my friends, is indeed one mole of an idea that needs to be whacked.

SPEED

The ride up the Millennium coaster was agonizingly slow with anticipation, and I needed to close my eyes to manage the terror rising in my throat. As I felt the car beginning to crest, I opened them wide so I could take in every second. For 30 seconds, I felt a rush that was unbelievable; 93 mph will do that for ya! With my feet back on solid ground, I was ready to hit every coaster in the park, feeling invincible and ready to feel the thrill all over again. Julie and her crowd of gal pals took off for the next big thrill, while my friend, Patty, who had chosen to join the fun, was not interested in risking her life again. We managed to find a middle ground and enjoy the rest of the day, though I kept staring at different coasters wondering how I could talk her into riding them. It got me thinking a lot about speed and how fast or slow we all move through life. If we go too fast we may miss something interesting and if we go too slow, we may get lapped. So what exactly is the right pace?

I watch Julie, at 18, racing into adulthood like it will only last a day. She's moving full tilt to establish her identity and independence. She was 18 for less than 24 hours before she was in the tattoo parlor, permanently marking her foot with Bob Marley song lyrics. I want to tell her to slow down, that she has plenty of time. I get that she wants to soak up every experience, every opportunity, but some of my favorite evenings are the ones just sitting quietly on my sister's patio, next to the fire pit with a bottle of wine. The peace on those evenings is intoxicating and is always a good reminder that life is well lived at all speeds.

Too often, I feel a sense of urgency to get things accomplished. I measure the success of my day by how much I get done. Even when I take time off from work, I have a list of projects to do and feel guilty if I take time to do nothing. I sometimes feel restless if I don't have a plan and I can get aggravated if I sleep too long. I keep a speedometer on my bike so I can monitor how fast I pedal to gauge my progress and people complain I walk too fast. Part of me feels I spent the better part of my adult life just standing still, and now that I have legs, I just want to move! Where is it that I'm headed to in such a hurry? Is this rushing around an attempt to get where I'm going, or to avoid living in the moment?

38

If it's true that I am rushing towards something, I have to believe that it is my quest to re-define my life. I sometimes feel that whatever happens next is within my control and I just need to go get it. Every moment spent in a new experience holds the possibility of a new passion or a new direction. If I'm not out there looking, it could be missed. On the other hand, if moving fast is my way of running from my past, then I have to believe that it's also the quest to re-define my life. I'm no longer someone's wife and the hours I spend parenting are about to be cut. So where does that leave me? Why do I have the sense that my life needs re-defining? Shouldn't I be accepting of what my life is right now in this place? "Yes!" is the resounding answer.

When I consider the people in my life who seem content, who are not racing through this life, the common thread is that they wake up each day already accepting what the day is going to bring. That does not mean that they don't hit bumps in the road; it does mean that they accept the path they walk on this day. Tomorrow may bring a new direction, but for today they accept where they are. Sometimes life might require them to run, and sometimes it means that they just may sit their ass down and take in the quiet moments, lingering with their own thoughts. These friends don't question the pace of the journey, or even where the journey is headed. They just accept wherever they are in the moment.

I'm 54 years old and I think maybe 54 mph is the right speed for me at this time. It doesn't take a lot to slow down, and I have room to speed up. Some days I can put on the brakes and on some I can fly with abandon. On other days, I can simply put on the cruise control and enjoy the ride. With my eyes wide open.

LIMITS

I think one of the worst feelings in the world is when you are driving along and all of a sudden you see the flashing lights behind you. That feeling in the pit of your stomach, until you find out if the lights are meant for you, is enough to ruin the song on the radio. I have often wondered how speed limits are determined. I mean, what makes 35 safer than 40? Or 60 safer than 70? As a driver, I have often pushed the posted limits believing I would only get stopped if I were exceeding the limit by more than 10 mph. This past week I learned that while there may be physical limits to my body, there are none when it comes to friendship.

My cycling team is made up of five diverse women, who generally know when to quit. Riding together over the last few years, we have seen each other exhausted, frustrated, and without make up. We signed up for a 50 mile ride with "gently rolling hills" to celebrate the 50th birthday of one member, and to train for a longer ride later in the month. As is the norm, I stayed hydrated for days before the ride, got plenty of rest, and prepared to tackle the route. I can only say that this route will forever be known as "the ride from Hell". Who knew that "gently rolling" actually meant over 25 miles of hills that reached straight up to the heavens? Sure, flying down steep roadways at 34 mph was a thrill, but overall, it was brutal, hot, and physically punishing. I pushed on, reminding myself that I had an out. Waiting at the half way point was a train. For a small fee, this silver bullet would transport any rider and bike back to the starting line. Hmmm.

Approaching the turn-around, waiting at a stop light, I fell over. With one foot clipped into the pedal, I lost my balance and found myself staring up at the team. That was the tipping point. I was either getting a ride back to the finish or going to take a less challenging route. The flat one. But after some fruit and fresh water I decided to buck up. If my teammates could do it, so could I, the regrets would lay heavy if I quit. As we made the first turn back on the course we faced a hill that drained my spirit as quickly as it had just been lifted. I felt old, fat, and tired. I stopped and looking at my teammates announced I was done. I had reached the limits of my endurance. How exactly did I get to the flat route, the quitter's route?

Each of my fellow riders tried not to laugh as they announced that the easy route started at the top of that hill, and one way or the other I was going to have to get there. I paused only momentarily before I stomped off. I started walking up that hill angry and feeling sorry for myself. The swear words were screaming through my brain and I could feel the tension building. I was angry at myself for agreeing to do the ride and angry at my younger teammates for seeming to have an easier time. But they also all walked up that hill and gave me the space to figure out what I could do. They made it clear that there was no shame in changing course; that I needed to do what was best for me.

Once at the top, I climbed back on my bike and began to pedal. I rode and cried as I thought of how discouraged I was by the limits of my body. When exactly had I become old? When exactly had I become someone who gave up? My dear teammates recognized that I needed to push through that wall by myself and hung back. I rode past the entrance to the easy route, choosing to keep my commitment, and pedaled alone for a few miles. But I could see my four friends in my rearview mirror and I knew they had my back. Slowly I began to feel better, stronger. The mental wall of frustration was crumbling, even though the last 30 miles were not any easier than the first 25. At different points we all needed to walk those hills and whoever got to the top first, waited until the whole team arrived.

The day was a great reminder that we don't always see the challenges that might be just over the next hill. We can plan and train for what we think is coming, but we never really know what might be ahead. We just have to be ready to keep pedaling until we can once again cruise with less effort. Will I do this particular ride again? Not a chance in Hell! Today I felt the limits of both my body and my thinking. I was lucky to be with people who would not let me give in to either.

A bottle of champagne was waiting at the finish line. Five friends, collapsed on the grass, sipped the bubbly right out of the bottle. We were hot, exhausted, and victorious! As we packed up our bikes and loaded into our separate cars, I couldn't help but think that, with these women, this team, there are no limits.

TANDEM

On long bike rides I like having partners. It breaks up the monotony and serves as motivation when someone is getting weary. Riders take turns with the lead, setting the pace. Those behind can still go at whatever speed is best for them, but at regular intervals everyone catches up and is in the same spot at the same time. Conversation is limited to when it's safe to ride side by side, which allows for both a shared experience and private time. Lately I've been fascinated by the number of tandems I see around town. I've seen couples, teenage girls, and parents with children all happily riding together on one bike. The idea of sharing the ride on one bike is both appealing and appalling to me at the same time. I wonder what that says about me and relationships.

Watching the tandem riders, I think about whether I would prefer riding in front or in the back. I like the idea of sitting behind someone and just taking in the scenery. It looks relaxing and like less work. Talk about cruise control. Of course, the front rider seems to have all the power. They get to steer, determine the speed and have a better view! A rather complicated system of communication and coordination, tandem cycling assumes that both riders trust the other to do their fair share. My Lord! What looks like fun is suddenly work and sounds a lot like marriage.

Most times, I'm happy with my single life. I've grown accustomed to handling things on my own or getting help from a group of good and dear friends. It's amazing to me how smart my friends are, and with a few tools, almost anything can be fixed. I have company when I want and am alone when need be. I can now go to the movies by myself and am quickly learning to cook for one. This summer, I've been busy with roller coasters, golf, comedy clubs, and theater. I was surprised, then, by some odd feelings that hit this past weekend, leaving me feeling a bit melancholy. Emotions were building, causing me to reflect on my life, and now were demanding my attention. They just happened to come smack in the middle of Julie's graduation party.

There I was, surrounded by family and close friends. The people who have supported Julie and me during our roughest patches. After almost 30 years, the two friends I've known the longest were actually meeting for the first time! The crowd included both happily married couples and several single friends.

Julie was busy with her friends and was particularly gracious in her interactions with the adults. I observed her becoming the young woman who has been floating around the edges of her adolescence. Yet, at several different moments, I felt very much alone. I flitted around the party making sure that my guests were being taken care of, but I was really looking for a way to figure out where I belonged. Oh don't get me wrong, I had a great time watching people I love laugh and enjoy the evening. I loved listening and telling stories, and I know they all hold me in their hearts as much as I hold them in mine.

As I watched folks head home, I began to dread the idea of not having someone with whom I could ride home and talk about how the night had played out. I felt sad that there was not someone to take it all in with and to say "we did it". I didn't get to climb into bed letting someone else know that they would have to be the one to return all the tables and chairs! I wasn't missing Julie's dad as much as I was missing feeling connected to someone in a very intimate way. It isn't that I don't appreciate my alone time, I just want to balance that with time shared in a relationship. I want to be able to keep riding by myself, and yet sometimes let someone else steer. I don't always want to pedal alone.

As I cleaned up and got re-organized, I kept thinking about those tandem riders. What makes that work? What keeps the riders balanced and in sync? How do they decide who is in front and who is in back? Mostly, how do they decide to take the ride together? I didn't come up with any answers, but I did get all the tables and chairs returned.

WATER

Shortly after our mother died, my younger sister and I went to stay with a maternal aunt for the summer. Overwhelmed with the prospect of caring for his young children, Dad decided that we should spend time with relatives who would care and nurture us in our time of loss. Aunt Irene, my mother's sister, lived right across the street from our paternal grandparents, so Barbie and I were lovingly looked after by both sides of the family. I have only vague memories of that summer; but I do remember playing Cootie and Mr. Potato Head with my cousin Jane as well as my grandfather's love of chewing tobacco.

What I remember most is falling into the deep end of a pool and not being able to swim. We were spending the day at my aunt's golf club and I was walking the edge of the water, staring at the bottom, curious. Suddenly I was in over my head! I remember a brief feeling of panic, although I was underwater for less than 10 seconds before being pulled out. This incident did not scar me or result in a fear of swimming. I only remember being drawn to the water in a very profound way.

I didn't even come close to drowning that day but lately feel I'm barely keeping my head above water. I once again feel as if I've fallen into the deep end, only this time, no one is pulling me out. As I kick my way to the surface, I feel weighed down by the memories of Julie's childhood and her impending departure. I've deluded myself into thinking that her actual leaving would somehow get delayed.

Yes, I know that Julie moving on to college is normal and healthy. Yes, I know that I will eventually enjoy this new found freedom. Yes, I know that millions of mothers survive this every day. Blah, blah, blah. Right now I'm simply grieving the loss of her need for me. It will pass but not without a bit more anxiety on my part. Julie's future is bright and full of promise and she's going to manage just fine without me. Part of my heart rejoices that she is ready and the other part is looking for how to fill this sense of emptiness that stalks me! For me, the world is not rotating on a normal axis; it feels out of whack and I'm struggling with the feeling that my life is out of order. I decided to do what I always do when I feel nuts: clean.

I scrubbed floors and toilets. I dusted every surface in the house. I vacuumed rugs and rotated the mattress. I cleaned cupboards and closets and threw out more than I kept. I cleaned out the freezer and stocked the fridge with healthy foods. This ordering of my physical world almost always seems to order my thinking and emotions. Not this time. As I sat on the couch looking at my sparkling floors, my sense of helplessness was no less and the sense of being in over my head was still with me. Then it began to rain; a long, slow, soft rain that reminded me of the healing power of water.

For as long as I can remember, being near water immediately calms my soul. In times of distress I often find myself at the beach, just looking at the horizon or walking the water's edge. The rhythmic sound of the waves is like a song that nurtures my heart. I suddenly felt pulled to the shore, and so I headed to the lake to let the music of the waves wash over me. Standing there, I was reminded of both the gentleness and the strength of water and how it can wear down the sharp edges of broken bottles to create beautiful pieces of beach glass. As each wave came in, I watched as it took a little bit more of life's chaos back out to sea to smooth out the rough parts.

I returned home to a clean house and a calmer soul. I was reminded that when I take care of myself, I can see more clearly and am better able to make sense of life's complications. I can also see the inherent abilities in those I love. Julie is a beautiful swimmer and not in danger of drowning. Yes, a major change is just days away. But I need to remember that if we give in to the strength of the water it will always carry us gently to the surface.

ANGELS

Probably the worst injury I endured was when I fell through our deck and landed 15 feet below onto a slab of concrete. There was a hole in the flooring that was being repaired, and I tried to step over it to walk down the steps to visit with neighbors. I was briefly knocked out and needed to be transported by ambulance to the hospital. Unbelievably, my only injury was a cut on the back of my head that required a few stitches. For days I couldn't walk without assistance, take a shower on my own, or even sit up for very long. I was one big bruise and was fortunate to have neighbors and friends who were there to get me back on my feet. It took a long time for the wounds to heal, and even now I'm convinced that some periodic back pain is a result of that fall. I also know that it could have been much worse: my husband had, only a few moments earlier, removed several boards with protruding nails from the very spot I landed.

My guardian angels were there that day, and I am counting on them now. My mother Virginia, grand-mother Clara, and great-aunt Winnie, have been saving my ass for years. I rely on their spirits to guide me during painful times. These strong ancestral women pack a powerful punch working together and, more than once, they've let me know of their presence. Virginia gave me life, Clara gave me her stubbornness, and Winnie blessed me with her sense of acceptance. Not bad as ancestors go. Definitely not bad as angels.

I've long believed that each of us is given a challenge or issue that we confront in different forms in this life. For me, it is loss. It started with that unimaginable childhood devastation, and I have only snippets of memories of my mother. The ones I do have are powerful and clear: the buttons on her coat, building a snowman, seeing her wave from a hospital window, are all images that are vivid to me.

Then there is nothing. I don't remember being told she died. I don't remember the funeral; I have been told that I actually refused to go. I don't remember the next couple of years. There are large gaps in my memory during which time I started kindergarten, had my tonsils out, and went to my father's wedding. I confronted those feelings of loss again and again during my years of miscarriages and the demise of my marriage.

All those experiences are exploding in my heart as I help pack up Julie for college. I'm feeling the pain of all those losses and the combination is overwhelming. I'm an open wound and the silliest things can set me off. A hot flash or running out of milk or spilling something on my shirt have all reduced me to tears in the last few days and I find myself simply exhausted. I feel as if I'm again falling through that hole in the deck and I'm looking for my angels to catch me. Fortunately, I realized I have a few here on earth.

I was having dinner with five of my best friends when Julie stopped by to bid them all farewell. Over the past four years, these women have served as surrogate mothers. They have each watched over Julie, and their extra eyes have comforted me just as their extra arms have comforted her. I listened as they joked with her that in just a few short days she would have no curfew. They cautioned her about grain alcohol punch and told her to study hard and play safely. Giving us both a gift, they sent Julie their cell numbers, with the instructions that, if she were ever in trouble, to call one of them before she calls me. They committed themselves to serve as a buffer should she ever need one. I cried as I listened to these women care for my daughter by removing the board with the protruding nails. Virginia, Clara, and Winnie are alive through them and continue to have my back.

Tomorrow we are off. I imagine the trip home will be harder than the trip down. I imagine my wounds will be raw and I will experience a bit of pain. But the road home is paved with all the women in my life who nurture and sustain me. Not just the five who were at dinner, but my sisters and dear friends who know my soul. Together, they can soften the blow. Together, they will help me heal and get back on my feet. Not bad as friends. Definitely not bad as angels.

BABY

Shortly before Julie was welcomed into our family, my former husband and I had scheduled a vacation to the Napa Valley. Flights had been booked, tours reserved, and new bathing suits purchased. Setting up a nursery with only 24 hours' notice left us reeling with the adjustments of parenting. Rather than cancel the trip, we decided we needed the time to breathe deeply and reconnect. Two grandmothers were more than excited to share in the care of Ms. Jules and, even though I knew she'd be well cared for, I wept when I left her with Mom and headed to the airport. At that point I'd been a parent for exactly 93 days, and I phoned every four hours to make sure Julie was OK. My baby!

I couldn't help but recall that trip as we packed the car with everything Target sells for a dorm room. For weeks the laundry room had been "college central" as we bought sheets, a comforter, toiletries, and laundry soap. We collected dishes and silverware, copier paper, and shower shoes. Never once did I consider that we could've avoided it all by making one large trip to Walmart when we arrived! Once we strapped the futon, still in the box, to the roof of the SUV, we were ready to roll. This was big.

Keeping in mind that I'm a college counselor and have advised hundreds of families to ready themselves for this exact moment, I was surprised by my own lack of preparation. For weeks I faked excitement and smiled as we shopped and organized. We talked about roommate issues, course selections, and meal plans. I recall telling other parents that it's a huge leap of faith to believe that our values are indeed in their heads and hearts; that our daughters are ready. But at night, alone in my bed, the fear and doubts would creep in. Had I taught my daughter all she needs to know? Will she hear my voice when she is questioning what to do? Was she ready...was I?

Despite the divorce, Julie's father and I chose to put aside our differences and share this experience, making the trip to campus together. A four hour car ride found us reviewing not only the entire contents of the car, but past vacations and holiday memories. It was eerily familiar as we slipped into our previous roles as a connected family. Past disappointments and divisions were put aside for this momentous experience. Periodically, one of us would slip in a life lesson and advice on how to manage the first days/weeks of college.

When I got close to being emotional, Julie simply patted my shoulder, plugged in her iPod, and sat back.

The restlessness began to creep into my bones about an hour from campus. The tightness in my throat was uncomfortable as we approached the dorm. Stepping out of the car, I found my legs shaky with the weight of this trek. Yet I forced my brain to switch to "take charge" mode and focused on hauling box after box up three flights of stairs. Already setting up the room was Tiffany, a high school friend with whom Julie had decided to share the 12' x 9' space. With her parents already working to unpack, the six of us set about arranging the furniture, thinking we could somehow make the cramped quarters larger. I found myself not really wanting to talk much as I felt my time with Julie was being invaded. I longed for the chance to be alone with her, to help her make the bed and give her that last piece of necessary wisdom. Once space was made, we all stared at that boxed futon. Out came the tool box and, fortunately with two dads, it was quickly assembled and under the window.

Soon enough it was time to find a place for a last meal and to pick up, believe it or not, a few last things at the store. Choking down a cheeseburger at the local diner, I felt the panic settling in for a visit. How would do I do this? How would I say good-bye? How would I get in that car? Julie, always one to surprise me, simply said, "Well, Mom, I'm going to be fine. Will you?" Her acknowledgement of my dilemma was enough to keep me from losing it over the french fries! She gently put her head on my shoulder, allowing me to wrap her up for a few moments. We lingered quietly for a bit longer and walked back to her new home. A quick check to make sure her towels were correctly folded was the last stall I could think of before it was time to leave.

For the first hour of the return trip, Julie's dad and I sat in silence, both reflecting on our individual concerns and fears. We didn't need words to know that, for the moment, we again shared a connection long buried. For that hour, our issues didn't exist...only two parents who knew that life would never be the same. It was the same thought we had 18 years earlier when we learned we would be parents. The rest of the trip home was light chit-chat designed to keep us from focusing on our mutual worries.

Surprisingly, it took longer than I expected for my tears to begin to escape. Arriving home, the silence was blaring. My eyes were wet as I wandered the empty rooms for a few moments before being brave enough to actually open Julie's bedroom door. I stood, taking in the shelves containing childhood trinkets and high school memorabilia. She had left those things behind, ready to collect new treasures. I briefly flashed ahead to the good cleaning the room would get the next day, but pushed that out of my mind to linger over the crate of stuffed animals.

I walked across the hall to my own room, not sure how I was going to get any sleep. There was no grandmother to call to make sure she was OK; no wine tour to distract me from my concerns. Flipping on the light, I saw a piece of paper on my pillow that had not been there the last time I was in the room. Picking up the note, I found a poem written by Miss Jules, a surprise gift for me. In part it read:

"I have responsibilities
And have to face my fears
For the rest of my years.

I am clueless
But there's one thing I know
My Mother is there
And loves me so."

Now, there was no stopping the tears. I laid on the bed, reading her words, touched by her gift, knowing she was in the right place…for her…for now. I let the feelings of loss and worry settle in, no longer feeling the need to fight them. I allowed myself to cry until I was just plain exhausted, falling asleep in my jeans. I slept deeply, too tired to dream.

My first thought in the morning was to reach for the phone…to call and check on her, just like when we traveled to Napa. Pausing, I put it back down. I realized Julie was a young adult starting her life and didn't need me to check every four hours. My baby was going to be ok. And as soon as I cleaned that room, so would I.

QUILTS

When that charming (idiot) golf pro told me to find a new hobby, I took up quilting. I was living on the edge of Amish country so the culture was ripe with opportunity. I met Janet who ran a quilt shop out of her home and was immediately hooked. For the next few years, before Julie, I always had a project going. With Janet as my coach, I made big quilts, wall quilts, and miniature pieces of art. I made baby gifts and Christmas stockings. I had yards of fabric, several styles of frames, and lots of spare time. My favorite part was selecting the fabric to cut into small pieces that were sewn together to form a pattern. Initially, I was horrible at blending fabric patterns, but I soon learned to love browsing Janet's shelves exploring all the options. I hated cutting the pieces, but loved sewing them together. I struggled with learning how to mark the design and do the initial basting, but I loved sitting for hours on end making rows of tiny stitches. It was peaceful, therapeutic, and allowed my creative side to flourish. I soon came to appreciate all the different steps and phases of creating a quilt and felt nurtured by the creativity.

Once Julie came along, I slowly began to withdraw from quilting. Projects took longer to complete and trips to Janet's shop occurred less often. My time was focused on parenting, and my creative needs were channeled into Halloween costumes and birthday cakes. After a couple of relocations, my sewing machine rarely came out and my frames were stowed away. With my last move, I packed away all the patchwork, thinking I would eventually pass them along to Julie, and donated yards and yards of fabric to a local school. This weekend, as I started to examine the pieces of my life, I found myself looking at a number of stored quilts and was reminded of what I loved about stitching.

For me, quilting is all about separate parts coming together to make one whole. It's about taking scraps and creating something beautiful. It's about taking all the layers and stitching them together to create something useful. Quilting evokes images of women gathering together to share their talents and their life stories. Passed from generation to generation, quilts have wrapped families in the warmth of their history. I learned that the Amish always put a mistake in every quilt because of their belief that nothing of this earth is perfect. My first quilt was a wall hanging with a simple pattern that's now faded from sunlight. The stitches are long, uneven and show my lack of skill. I love that piece because it was my first. I spent hours making those uneven stitches and felt a tremendous sense of pride when it was completed. It wasn't perfect but it was beautiful. Like Julie.

My daughter is much like a quilt. She is a collection of beautiful "colors" that together tell a story. She has multiple layers that make up the whole of her experiences. I've given Julie part of her history but it's now time for her to create the pattern. As she settles into college life, her story is only beginning to take shape. She has so many choices in front of her, and she must decide what works and what to include. Julie is now the one who will stitch those pieces together. I expect that she will pick colors and patterns different from what I would select, but I need to let her browse those same shelves, and to choose her own experiences to find what works best.

It's time for me to do the same. I have the opportunity to start a new quilt with new colors and new patterns. The prospect is both exciting and daunting and I must admit I'm a bit frightened by the possibilities. Stored away in the front hall closet is some beautiful fabric that I didn't give away. I have all I need to make a covering with stunning colors and rows of tiny stitches. Like the Amish, I'm sure the finished work won't be perfect. I'm equally sure that "peace" in this new life will be found among the scraps. Piece by piece, I will find it.

PINK

My favorite part of going to the movies is the previews. The trailers tease us with the most dramatic moments, the most exciting chases, and the funniest lines. I love getting a glimpse of what's coming and being able to decide if it's a film I want to see. The shorts give an idea of the theme of the movie, but rarely hint at the ending. What a great idea! So recently, in keeping with the thought that maybe there is a life plan for all of us, I began to wonder what would happen if life gave each of us a sneak peek. If it did, would we choose to skip any part that awaited us? If we knew exactly what pain or joy was coming, is that a trailer you would want to see? I wonder if our choices in this life set the course for the plan, or does the plan set the groundwork for our choices?

One of the few memories I have of my mother is of her leaving to go to the doctor. She leaned over, kissed me, saying she would be back soon. It was the last time I remember seeing her. That memory has, at times, comforted me, and at other times haunted me. My life was permanently impacted. I've spent much of my adult life believing that at some point, genetics would catch up and I too would have breast cancer. I celebrated turning 30 because it meant that I had lived longer than she, and I often give thanks that neither of my sisters, or myself, have had more than the occasional scare.

Unfortunately, I've spent way too much time trying to live as if I could control what comes next. I can be terrible at taking each day as it comes, and too often I want the answers even before I have all the questions. This weekend, as I again took part in the Race for the Cure, I found myself really beginning to understand what it means to live in the present.

I was surrounded by people walking in support of the millions of those whose lives have been impacted in some way by this disease. I realized that although sad, my experience is not unique. I walked behind young men participating in memory of their wives. I walked behind women wearing bandanas to cover their baldness, while at the same time, pushing strollers. I walked next to people with too many names of deceased loved ones on their backs, and I walked with an ever growing number of men who were holding the hands of women they love. As one shirt proclaimed, "Men have a breasted interest". I walked in memory of my mother but also walked beside my dear sweet friend, Barb, wearing a t-shirt identifying her as survivor. This incredible woman is a mother, grandmother, sister, and friend. She fought this hideous disease with beauty and grace and won! She looks stunning in pink.

Friends who love Barb marvel at how she takes each day, each moment, with whatever it brings. At her core, she's at peace with her life, and her home reflects the serenity that she's found. She has tremendous faith that she's always exactly where she is supposed to be and this faith guides her every day. This serenity only illuminates her beauty and people are drawn to her in a very profound way. I often feel envious of Barb's ability to live in the present and her acceptance that the past is something to be learned from, not lived in. When I've asked her how she has learned to really take each day as it comes, her response is always the same: she chooses to.

During the walk, I paid attention to the number of women wearing pink shirts and those walking in celebration of a loved one who has fought and won. My mother suffered in the 1950's, a time when treatment options were limited. While today, far too many women are still suffering, far more are surviving. The sheer number of people participating was overwhelming and I paid attention to the sounds of laughter and applause that surrounded the racers. I saw mothers dancing with their children. I watched as men wrapped the ladies they love in warm hugs. I cheered as my friend finished the walk by joining hundreds of others in pink shirts crossing the finish line. Yes, I grieved for my mother, but I rejoiced for women I know who have bravely fought and won.

For three miles, I thought about staying connected to the past versus being tied to it. We aren't guaranteed an easy life and despite my wish for a preview, I'm not sure I want to know what comes next. I **am** sure that if there is ever a time to embrace this life I've been given, now is that time. Is there a plan for each of us? I choose to believe there is, but I'm not sure it matters. What matters is what we do with it. Barb chooses to wake up each day with a sense of hope and gratitude. I think I will join her on that walk as well.

FLYING

When I was about 8-years old, I went on my first airplane ride. My father had a pilot's license and he took me flying in his little twin engine Cessna. He told me we had flown to Canada and I, of course, immediately bragged to my older siblings about my adventure. They laughed at me, knowing that in a 45 minute flight, there was no way dad had flown me to Canada and back. I was outraged at their disbelief but equally adamant in my own belief that my dad would not lie to me. I fell deeply in love with flying, and even though subsequent flights are not as memorable, I frequently took flight in my dreams.

I'm beyond lucky to experience flying dreams. In these, I can literally flap my arms and take off! I can soar above the earth with ease and coast for hours. The sense of taking off is intense and real. The sun is always shining and I'm free to look at the world and all the people I love. The sense of freedom I experience is unbelievable, and I awake with joy in my heart. I'm lucky enough to have these flying dreams several times a year, and was sad to learn that not everyone is so lucky. I've actually learned that a lot of people I know have never had even one flying dream. When I fly in my sleep, everything is clear for miles; everything makes sense. There are no clouds blocking my view and I know exactly where I'm going. Maybe that's what makes it a dream.

This past week, on flights to and from St. Louis, I was reminded that, as a passenger, I have absolutely no control over the flight. I can choose to get on the plane or not. Once buckled in, I'm going wherever the plane goes. As I looked out the window, I had no idea where I was or how close I was to my destination. I watched for breaks in the clouds so that I could see the ground, see that I was headed somewhere! I had to trust that the pilot knew what he/she was doing, and that I would land safely. Again I found myself wondering if the life path I'm now on is the right one, if there is indeed a flight plan.

With Jules now safely planted in the dorm, I am acutely aware of being alone. I'm adjusting to this role as an empty-nester with hesitancy and a bit of fear. I think about inviting people into my life, but I realize how scared I am to open up to someone new and to again trust someone with my heart. The damage caused by marital betrayal runs deep. Friends and family keep encouraging me to be open to new experiences and new relationships, and I am constantly asked if I have "met anyone". I worry that even if I do, I might just have too much baggage. When I was in my 20's, that baggage was a carry-on; now it's probably well over the checked bag limit! I wonder if I'm capable of trusting anyone enough to risk sharing even a small part of my life, let alone a lifetime. But if I'm honest with myself, I do want to take that chance. I want to experience again the sense of getting to know someone's fears and joys. And of sharing mine.

This doesn't mean that I'm unhappy with my life now; it doesn't mean I think something is missing. It does mean that I believe my life could be enhanced by allowing myself to trust. Being alone does not create loneliness; feeling afraid is what makes me feel lonely. A tiny voice keeps telling me that I am ready to take the first step. The challenge is to balance the hurt of the past with the hope of the future.

I'm clueless about how to begin. How does a woman my age start exploring new relationships? The thought of dating is scary enough without a lesson in learning to trust. I don't mean putting my faith into someone else as much as I mean learning to rely on my own judgment. For that I definitely need a flight plan; I don't want to again find myself lost in the clouds.

I think I need to start with simply embracing the idea. What would it be like to share time and experiences with a man again? Am I content and confident enough in my own life to invite someone in? I have questions, but no answers. I want to find out.

In my dreams, I know exactly where I am and I take off with abandon. In my waking moments, I have huge doubts as to whether or not I'm going to move in the right direction and land safely. The reality is that Dad didn't fly me to Canada on that inaugural flight. But he knew where he was going and how to get there. Maybe I need to ask him for flight lessons.

FLASHES

During a recent thunderstorm, I had a flashback to Jules being about four years old. The first crack of thunder would cause her to fly into our bedroom to hide under the covers. Rather than shield her from the noise, I would take her hand and sit on the porch to watch the storm. Some of the lightning flashes were brilliant in their displays of light and electricity, and she learned to be fascinated instead of frightened. I need to remember those storms as I confront issues of aging. I'm intrigued and worried by the physical changes that are occurring. Remembering thunderstorms with Julie has me thinking a lot about all the flashes in my life and feeling a bit old.

At times I feel my life has happened in a flash. I'm old enough to remember seeing "Flashdance" at the movies. I have actually used the term "flash in a pan", and I can recall being a Kent State "Golden Flash" in the years when they never won a game. But nothing in this life has prepared me for menopausal hot flashes! What an appropriate term for those sudden bolts of heat that begin at the waist and shoot up to my hairline, leaving me feeling like I was hit by molten lava!

It seems like such a cliché to complain about this symptom of aging. As an adolescent and young adult, I would make fun of women complaining about this affliction. I couldn't imagine ever being old enough to have the experience, and I was sure that I'd mature without ever having even a lukewarm burst. Now I find myself resolved to throwing off the covers, opening the window, and rolling over onto a cold pillow without ever getting up. I'm equally annoyed that I have to close the window and sink back under the comforter two minutes later, repeating the pattern several times in the course of one night. On the rare occasion that I actually sleep through, I wake up thanking a God that I'm sure is a man because a female would never have cursed women this way!

Yes, there are medical treatments for this malady, but the reported side effects discourage me from exploring them further. I can endure these annoying shifts in temperature for whatever time it takes for my body to re-adjust my personal thermostat. More importantly, I have to figure out how to re-adjust my thinking about aging. As I approach yet another birthday, I wonder what it means to age without being old. And old is what I'm feeling. I don't like how I look, I don't like what I wear, and I have an unrealistic view of how I should behave. I'm once again avoiding the camera's flash because I don't like the image that will be captured. I've always assumed I do not look my age, but more and more people seem to know exactly how old I am. What I see in the mirror IS exactly what others see; can I be ok with that? Or do I need to redefine how I view myself?

The other night, while strolling through an art district with a friend, I almost bought a leopard print coat in a re-sale shop. I thought it would be a fun piece to wear from time to time but it was just a tad too small. My friend thought it looked great, but when I described it to my adult nieces the next day, they both rolled their eyes and looked grateful it hadn't fit. I was momentarily relieved that I had resisted the temptation and just as quickly disappointed for not doing something that made me feel good. I seem to follow a path of what's appropriate for someone my age rather than embracing the idea that with age comes the freedom to not fit in. The freedom to not care so much about the opinions of others. It comes with the freedom to no longer worry that I might not fit someone else's image. Mostly it comes with the freedom to question myself less. I'm the only one who needs to be happy with me. If relieved of the burden of worrying about the expectations of others, age is no longer an issue. In a flash of insight, I decided to follow my instincts more and when I can, add a bit of funk to my world.

Julie learned to embrace storms and actually loves to watch them come in over the lake. She frequently walks outside when she hears that first clap of thunder to watch the light show. I need to do the same with my age. Hot flashes don't mean old, tired, and dried up. They do mean wisdom, experience, and power. They mean I've earned the right to wear a leopard print if I wish. I might just go back and give myself the gift of that coat. Now there is a flash of brilliance!

DOROTHY

Dorothy Gale is my favorite movie character. As a kid, I loved the annual showing of the "Wizard of Oz". I waited in great anticipation for Dorothy to work through the dangers of the forest, battle the wicked witch, and find her way home. In graduate school, I once hosted a "Wizard of Oz" themed Halloween party and found my small apartment jammed with munchkins, the tin man, and even the yellow brick road! My dear friend, Jim, showed up minus a costume, announcing that he was Frank Baum, author of the "Wizard of Oz"! I entertained my guests as Dorothy, with poppies on the table and serving up apples. That party is a favorite memory from a time when every day brought new adventures and new friends.

Many years later, when Julie was eight, I duplicated my costume for her. I spent weeks perfecting each detail, including the hair ribbons, basket, and a tiny dog. Dressed up in her blue and white pinafore, with braids and ruby slippers, she went trick or treating. It was one of my favorite costumes; she looked perfect as she headed out the door. She returned from her travels, full of stories about the people she had met along the way. Julie may no longer be dressed up like Dorothy, but she is embarking on a journey that will take her through strange and wonderful lands.

When Dorothy left Kansas, she had no idea what awaited her. She only felt the pull toward something unknown, a need to learn about who she was, and where she belonged. In her mind and in her dreams, that place was over the rainbow. Julie has also gone looking for her heart's desire, but in her case, the Emerald City is South Dakota. It is there she feels drawn; it is there she feels she'll find answers to her questions. You see, on her own, Julie has found her birth family and is anxious to figure out where she belongs.

In the movie, everyone Dorothy encountered had an opinion about which direction she should go. Throughout her journey, Dorothy was helped by new friends, considered new ideas, but never strayed from her belief in what was right for her. When people or events tried to discourage or deter her, Dorothy stayed true to her own heart, knowing instinctively that she had to find her own way. She didn't leave anyone behind, choosing to share the journey with those who were also searching. Dorothy used the security of her past to help navigate the present in the hopes of a bright future. Julie started her journey solo but has rejoiced in sharing the news that she has, indeed, found those missing people in her life.

I know, as sure as the Good Witch Glinda knew, that Julie has the heart, the brains, and the courage for this adventure. What awaits her in South Dakota is anyone's guess and there are sure to be both rainbows and flying monkeys. Maybe Julie will find South Dakota as beautiful as Dorothy found the Emerald City. Then again, maybe she'll find the wizard to be just a man behind the curtain. I don't know. I do pray she heeds Glinda's advice to hold tight inside her ruby slippers, for their magic is powerful and will protect her wherever she goes. Just a few clicks and Julie will be able to determine what feels right.

When the path is confusing, when the trees are throwing apples, I will be there. I'll do whatever she needs to find her peace, to find her heart's desire. Like Glinda, I'll be in the background offering assistance when it is sought. And like Auntie Em, I will be right here when she needs a place to land.

WEIGHT

I hate the idea of exercising. I long to be naturally fit and need not to work at it. The older I get, the harder it is to keep up the pace. If I'm outside walking or riding my bike, I'm happy breathing in the smells of the seasons and feeling the air on my skin. But working out in a gym is so incredibly boring and tedious that I want to poke my eyes out; or at least throw the damn hand weights at the really fit 30-year old on the next machine over. The other day as I was pushing 90 pounds of brick shaped metal up on the shoulder press, I started to think of all the weight I carry as I watch Julie navigate the changes and challenge she is currently facing. Although I did not give birth to my daughter, I did promise to care for her as if I did; to give Julie a good life. Lately I have worried more than usual about whether I did it right.

When I got the call in June of 1992, that this 5 ½ pound infant could join my family, I didn't for one moment stop and think about what I was in for. Within 12 hours I boarded a plane and headed to South Dakota. I felt no doubt, no fear, no anxiety…only excitement. I didn't consider that I might be making a rash decision or that I should slow down. I only felt the pull to love this child, to be her mother. At that moment, I didn't truly understand, in my soul, the sacrifice her birth mother was making. We met, we talked, and I made an oath to her to care for her daughter. Remarkably, I was pretty cavalier about the process, feeling entitled to assume the role of mother. In retrospect, it was shameful, as the next day I left the hospital with too little thought of Julie's birth mother. After a whirlwind trip through Kmart for diapers, clothes and bottles, this tiny child and I began to get to know each other. I felt like a mom from the first moment I held her.

During that first week, Julie had an allergic reaction to her formula and was in pain. I immediately felt helpless to relieve her discomfort and wanted nothing more than for her to feel better. I felt responsible for giving her the formula that caused the distress and it was the beginning of years of wanting to take away any hurt. There is a part of me that feels responsible for all the anguish in Julie's life. I know of course, that I'm not, but such is the mentality of many of us as parents. As much as we know that with struggle comes growth, we want our children to experience minimal growing pains. Watching them learn the lessons of their lives is sometimes an incredibly heavy burden. Julie's burdens are my burdens; Julie's pain is my pain.

Being a mom is, at the same time, the best and hardest thing I've ever done. In my heart I have thanked Julie's birth mother every day for allowing me to be a mother. Can I tell her I did it right? Yes, I have loved and cared for Julie. Yes, I have tried to provide the best life for her. Yes, sometimes I struggled. I would love to change some of my parenting decisions and re-do times I know I caused Julie some amount of unhappiness. I also know that a life lived in regret is carrying unnecessary weight into the future. The reality is, it's now my turn to share Julie.

As we begin to plan a December trip to South Dakota to meet Julie's birth family, I again feel no doubts about getting on that plane. I do feel some anxiety and fear. Julie's birth mother watched as I walked out of the hospital with her daughter and I can't begin to imagine what she felt. There was no promise we would ever walk back into her life and she has waited, patiently, 18 years for this moment. She made room in her heart to let go and now I need to make room in mine.

On my first trip to South Dakota, I felt weightless on the plane. Nothing was holding me down or holding me back. This time the weight of emotions is enormous. I fear I'm not strong enough, that I haven't trained enough. Guess I better head back to the gym.

NOTHING

Every year at this time, I send an email to family and friends about all the things for which I am thankful. I do it mostly to remind myself of the many unbelievably wonderful moments of the past year. This year has been no different and I again approach the holidays wanting to give thanks. Only this year, I find myself wanting to give thanks for nothing.

I want to give thanks for being given nothing I can't handle. Oh, there were moments that brought me to my knees, but each time I managed to get back up and keep moving forward. Each experience made me stronger and wiser and gave me the insight to accept the next one. I'm guilty of feeling sorry for myself when life doesn't go the way I would like, but I'm pretty sure I would not change anything.

I can say that during this year there is nothing for which I feel ashamed. Yes, I have made mistakes; yes, I would like a do-over on some bad decisions; yes, I embarrassed myself on more than one occasion. There was one situation that caused me to make a pretty significant character adjustment. It wasn't painless, but necessary to make sure I don't make the same mistake again. I'm far from perfect, but do feel perfectly content with my beliefs and values.

I have learned that I feel nothing but respect for people who accept hardship without complaint: like the times I've been passed on a long bike ride by someone pedaling with a prosthetic leg. Suddenly being hot on that same ride becomes a concern of idiotic proportions. I'm quick to be selfishly concerned about my own physical comforts rather than think of how I can relieve the discomfort of others.

I feel nothing but bewilderment by this new love of writing. There's nothing in my past to suggest I would find pleasure in this process. I even entered a writing contest sponsored by a major magazine! I've found great peace in putting my ramblings down on paper and hearing from readers that I have touched some part of their heart.

I feel nothing but calm when I'm simply playing a game of cards with my dad. How lucky I am to be able to sit quietly with him, even when he is kicking my butt at gin. I also feel nothing but relief that Mom cares for him as he struggles with his physical limitations.

I have nothing but pride in Julie. I'm particularly honored that she continues to share both her joys and struggles with me. I was the first person she called after making contact with her birth family and the first person she called when the going got tough at school. I will always have her back and I will embrace all the people she chooses to love.

Although I sometimes feel lonely, I feel nothing but love from so many people. I may not be experiencing the intimacy provided by romance, but I've never felt there's no one to call when I'm distressed. I can honestly say that there was not one day this past year that I did not say or hear the words "I love you." Wow!

I feel nothing but gratitude for a life that has been blessed with so few real challenges. My life is rich with people who have made even those moments less difficult. And that is everything.

JOURNEY

When my sister, Nancy, was in town for Thanksgiving, she shared with me a toast our father gave on her 50th birthday. He wrote about Nancy's many journeys to "find herself" and how happy he was when she finally did. I flashed back to the moment I remember him muttering, "If she wants to find herself, she should just look down her shirt. She's right there." As I read the toast, I was impressed with his obvious patience with Nancy during those years. I didn't realize he was walking a fine line between holding her hand and holding her up. I do now.

It seems that every week Julie has some big announcement. Trust me when I say that finding her birth family is one of the smaller ones! I feel like an inflatable clown that just keeps bouncing back up whenever it gets knocked over! "Hey, mom...boom! Hey, mom...boom! Hey, mom..." well, you get the picture. I want to cut through all the crap and design her life for her! I want her to look down her shirt and see that everything she needs to know is already there! I know that college is a time to explore, test, fail, and get back up. I know that it's a time to figure out new relationships and new ways of thinking. I know with each experience, Julie is one step further in her journey toward self-awareness. What I don't know is why HER journey has ME so weary!

Over the last few months, I have often found myself on my knees in prayer, but don't feel like I'm finding the answers that I'm looking for. I've always believed in a higher power and I've always believed that there is a plan for my life. I have great faith that I'm guided in my journey by a spirit that is kind and loving. I've been blessed with an amazing ability to get back up when I have stumbled. What I'm missing at this moment in time is the faith that I will be able to handle the next challenge. I'd like to believe that at some point the road will get less complicated, even for a short period of time.

I'm not feeling sorry for myself. Well, maybe a little. I know in many ways my life has far fewer burdens than others carry. But I'd really like a break! I'm increasingly anxious about our trip to South Dakota. Can I be as open as I want to be? Can I embrace this family to whom Julie is already connected? Can I let go enough to let her find her way? What if it doesn't go well? What if Julie is hurt or disappointed? She has invested her heart and I worry she is too trusting. This past week, Julie and I were sorting through pictures of her childhood, creating a photo album for her birth mother. It was my idea; I felt it would be a good way for Julie to share some of her life stories. With each photo we selected, I felt I was losing a tiny bit of Julie. In some ways, this trip is about giving her back.

As we get closer to leaving, Julie gets more excited and I get more scared. I don't want to feel all the worry and fear by myself. Being a single mom, I don't feel strong enough, don't have faith that I can handle it alone; I want someone to hold me up when we're there. I'm trying to tap into the faith that has guided my life all these years, but right now I'm not feeling it. I need to before I get on that plane. The reality is that Julie is once again counting on me to be her support. She is counting on me to guide her because she has faith that I can.

Nancy traveled to Europe, Colorado, Florida, and several other spots before she found her peace on a ranch in Massachusetts. Her journey was full of detours and stop signs but ultimately, she found the route that was right for her. I need to remember that as I watch Julie take the steps to connect her past to her future. Like her Aunt Nancy, Julie is blessed with a sense of adventure and trust. Like her aunt, she will at times, feel lost. Like Nancy, I believe Julie will find her place and settle in. Just like Dad, I hope to find that **balance between holding her hand and holding her up.**

KALEIDOSCOPE

I can't remember a time I didn't love looking through a kaleidoscope. It is magical to turn the cylinder, and create endless designs of intersecting circles, squares, and triangles. When held up to the light, the mirror creates even more brilliant colors and arrangements. There is no end to the possibilities. This is the image that keeps coming to mind when I try to describe taking my daughter to meet her birth family.

The journey started 18 years earlier in Sioux Falls, on a Tuesday, where Julie was born. I got the call on Wednesday informing me adoption was possible. By Thursday, I was in South Dakota where I was blessed to meet Lori, a young woman who already knew the extent of her love for this child. It was this overwhelming love that was allowing me to become a mother. I promised Lori that her daughter would always know her history, always know how much she was loved. I promised that, although I was not responsible for bringing this child into the world, I would be responsible for bringing her up in it. I was willing to make these promises because I was thinking of my own needs, my own desire to share my love with a child. On Friday, I left the hospital with Julie and never looked back.

Over the years, Julie learned the details of her birth, and was often told how much she was loved by many people. Every Mother's Day, every birthday, I offered up a silent prayer of gratitude for Lori's gift. Although I meant every word, in my heart I hoped my love for Julie would be enough, that one mother would be enough. On more than one occasion I reminded my daughter how I would support seeking out her birth family. Each time she simply shrugged her shoulders and denied any interest. As a high school guidance counselor, I interpreted this to mean that Julie was content with her identity, she felt no conflict. What I failed to consider was maybe, just maybe, Julie might not share all of her feelings with me. Just maybe there was a tug at her heart telling her to explore her history, her story. What didn't occur to me was that she might wait until she was at college to begin the journey. Imagine my surprise and panic when I received that midnight call from her dorm room announcing not only had she found her birth family, she had just spoken to her brother. I realized the moment had arrived for me to again look Lori in the eye and tell her that I had indeed kept my promises.

As much as I wanted to slow down the process of meeting Lori and her two grown children, Josh and Claire, life had other plans. Josh, a young Marine, was going to be deployed to Afghanistan right after the holidays, and our window of opportunity was narrow. I struggled with the decision to either join Julie in meeting her family or let her go on her own. In the end, it was Julie who made the decision for me. "Why wouldn't I want you to come with me?" she asked. "Don't you want to see them again?" I silently had to admit my very real conflict. Of course I wanted to join her on this journey, but it meant facing my own fear of losing my place in her heart. When she was born, I couldn't get to South Dakota fast enough, and now I needed to do the same again. Reservations were made, there was no turning back.

We almost missed the plane. Two days after Christmas, the security checkpoints were moving slowly. I must admit the thought of delaying the trip was appealing, but Julie was working the line trying to move ahead. As we finished the screening, we had exactly 10 minutes until departure. Julie didn't even put her boots back on; she took off running. I knew in that instant that missing the plane wasn't an option. So I ran behind her, and we arrived at the gate seconds before they closed the door. As we settled into our seats, I looked at Julie and saw the relief wash over her. My anxiety was climbing faster than the plane, but she was calm and ready for a nap. While the pilot navigated the flight, I tried to navigate the maze of feelings that swirled within me. When we again hit the tarmac, I felt a jolt in my soul that loosened every emotion in my body: every joy, every sorrow.

As we began the hour drive from Sioux Falls, I was grateful for the vastness of the landscape. Our trip was 60 miles of open land dotted with the occasional barn or grain silo. With snow and ice covering the trees, the view was spectacular. The simplicity of nature kept reminding me of the simplicity of this trip. On both sides was love for this young woman. That realization, combined with the surrounding physical beauty, allowed me to calm the terror rising in my throat. I forced myself to breathe. In too little time, we were pulling up to the restaurant where we had agreed to meet Lori, Josh, and Claire. So many moments had brought us to this one, and I had no idea what to expect.

I watched as Julie and Lori cautiously approached each other. I stayed by the car, letting the drama unfold in front of me. The two of them stared at each other before embracing, and it seemed as if they were both trying to believe the moment was real. I paced, feeling too much like a voyeur, but having no place to go. After a few moments, Lori approached with tears in her eyes and threw her arms around me. "Thank you," she said as her tears flowed. "I knew you were the right one." In that moment, I turned the kaleidoscope to create a new design.

The next few days were a blur of emotional challenges that ranged from fear to sadness to acceptance. I was amazed by the similarities between Julie and her siblings: allergies, facial expressions, musical tastes, and attitudes toward life. Josh and Claire immediately fell into the role of playing big brother and sister, and they were eager to share their life stories and to learn of Julie's. My heart leapt with joy for Julie as I realized siblings would change her life forever. I quietly observed the connections being made and found a delicate balance between holding on and letting go.

It was over a mother-daughter dinner that the most interesting design was revealed. While eating Chinese, Lori, Claire, Julie, and I explored our new relationships with each other. Lori is a mom who has wondered every day if her daughter was safe and happy. She paused over each picture in the photo album Julie and I had created, trying to take in each moment. Claire, a kind soul who is balancing motherhood with her own dreams, admitted that, while she had not understood my joining Julie on this trip, she was now pleased I was there. She has wisdom and an innocence that is moving to experience. Julie was open in a way that I had not previously experienced, soaking up each new gem of information. I realized each of us contributed to the kaleidoscope in a unique way. Each of us was willing to open our hearts wide enough to let in the unexpected.

I watched as Julie basked in the glow of the attention and love. I could see her confusion and questions changing to understanding and acceptance. I could feel her anxiety lessening and her confidence growing. Her story was coming full circle. How could I not embrace the place and people responsible for Julie? How could I feel anything but gratitude for them allowing me to be a part of it? Am I worried about my place in Julie's life? No. Julie's heart is big enough for everyone. And for that, I should be proud. I learned that love, like a kaleidoscope, is made up of a million small jewels that can create a stunning and surprising life design.

Julie's birth family is a critical part of her life design. They bring different shapes and sizes and colors to the kaleidoscope and add to the beauty that is already there. The patterns that can now be created are stunning in their potential. The mirror that reflects their brilliance? That would be Julie.

WARRIORS

I know a number of people who I would consider to be warriors: women who have battled and beaten breast cancer; friends who are living full lives with HIV; my father, who's living with Parkinson's; individuals who have accepted life's challenges with no complaint. All are worthy of the title. I don't consider myself to be someone whom others would consider a warrior, but last week a good friend sent me a link to a website describing the "Warrior Dash". It's a 3-mile run that includes several interesting obstacles like crawling through mud, rappelling down a cliff, running up bales of hay, and jumping over fire. Not one to shy away from a physical or mental challenge, my friend was already signed up. I walked into her office and only two words came out of my mouth, "I can't." Only two came out of hers' "Why not?" A million words ran through my mind: too old, can't run, out of shape. But only one word stuck: "excuses". I wonder how often I say, "I can't" before I even let an idea settle into my consciousness.

I have never been one to feel I've accomplished very much in my life. Professionally, I've spent 30 years waiting for someone to figure out I really don't know what I'm doing! Thousands of people do what I do, I don't see myself as particularly brilliant. I'm always shocked when I'm told that some people find my confidence intimidating. Really? I'm so much more in awe of others' accomplishments than I am of my own. When a new opportunity presents itself, my first thought is reasons why I will fail; this isn't new to me. I started graduate school sure I would get booted. I didn't think I would make it through my second graduate program either. I never thought I'd survive my divorce, and riding a bike 150 miles in two days? Impossible! So why do I trivialize my abilities and make only safe choices? There are the obvious answers of being afraid of failure or fear of the unknown. I don't think either is accurate. I think I'm just lazy!

I love a challenge when it's quick and requires very little effort. I welcome competition when it's just show up and participate. I say I want to learn new things, but mostly I want the new experience and then want to move on to something else. Last summer, I spoke often of my desire to learn to play golf. I went once. I recently read about a 70+ year old nun who had just completed her third Iron Man Triathlon. HER THIRD! By comparison, jumping through a

71

few tires, climbing over some cars, and running through a wind tunnel in the Warrior Dash seems pretty tame. I'm going to have to train. I'm going to have to practice. It will require commitment and I wonder just how good I am at that!

Last year at this time, I remember thinking I want to define my life in more ways than as a mom. I put my focus on writing because I wanted to push myself to get better at it. The writing doesn't always come easily, but I stuck with it and now know I can do it. Words have given a voice to so many feelings and helped me through moments of confusion and transition. I now consider writing to be as much a part of me as brushing my teeth or walking the dog, a permanent part of my existence. So I **can** commit to things and this year I want to focus on thinking "I can" not I think "I can't."

It's time to add a new challenge. I think the Warrior Dash is just the ticket. I registered and I'm officially in training for the June event. Call me crazy, but I'm already having fun thinking of ways to get ready. I have to develop more upper body strength, but I'm pretty sure I do not have to train for the mud crawl! I may ultimately curse myself for getting into this, but you should see the super cool Warrior Viking hat you get for completing the run. For that, I can do anything!

HUMPTY-DUMPTY

I never really liked the nursery rhyme "Humpty Dumpty." The idea that something is so broken that it can't be put back together again always makes me sad, particularly since Humpty had "all the king horses and all the king's men" available to fix him. I've been told that my older sister once broke my nose. The story goes that I was sitting on the edge of the couch when Nancy pushed me off. I don't remember falling, but I have a flash of a memory of lying on a table with a doctor staring intently at my face. In the many years since, I've been fortunate not to break another bone but, lately, I'm being pulled in so many different directions that I feel stretched to the point of fracture. The demands of work, Julie, and my aging parents have all made my own perch on the wall a bit precarious. Although I'm not that worried about getting put back together, I'm again taking care of everyone else and not paying enough attention to what I need. Plus, the people I want to help don't see all the demands being made; they see only what they need.

I love my job. I'm good at it. Because I do it well, it's sometimes assumed that I can handle anything that gets thrown my way. Lately, a lot of extra things have been added to my plate and I'm afraid I'll end up doing a less than stellar job at all of them. I'm having difficulty finding a sense of balance. Even though I know over the next few weeks the expectations will even out, the increased stress level at work is occurring at a time when my empty nest is about to get both physically and psychologically a bit more crowded.

Julie's adjustment to college has been difficult and she has, on more than one occasion, spoken of wanting to return home. A year ago I was worried about defining my life in response to her leaving. I've now come to realize that when it comes to parenting the only thing that really changes about the job is the zip code! Her father, my ex-husband, is also returning to town and I know that he has expectations of me that I cannot meet. He's looking for a friendship that I'm not sure I can offer. Then there are my parents, who every day need a bit more care and attention. It's funny: Julie needs my help but doesn't want it; her father wants my help but shouldn't need it; my parents view help as just one more way they are losing their independence. I'm drowning in my desire to be what everyone else needs while figuring out where the line is between support and enabling, between enabling and compassion, between compassion and dignity.

Right now, these lines seem extremely blurry. Julie is in a dark place and needs me to both hold and shine the light until she can do it on her own. Her father refuses to see the light. My parents, well, they really need to feel some light still exists. After another health emergency and another week of wondering just how much more my father can take, I'm exhausted from the worry that comes when people you love are hurting. Surprisingly, as this difficult week comes to a close, I find myself fairly calm and finding ways to make sure that I don't crack. My nightly word puzzles, crocheting, and a new interest in running have all helped me get through the craziness of the last few months.

But the real issue looms large. How do I say "No" to people I love or have loved? When I think of my original desire to re-define my life, I fret that in many ways I'm in the exact same place I was a year ago. I don't know that I've claimed the sense of independence I sought or learned how to let others struggle on their own. I feel like my past is chasing me, and I don't know how to get free. My empty nest journey is taking a major detour, and my enabling ways are in the car right behind me. I'm learning how critical it is to not assume what someone else needs. As a life-time enabler, I'm guilty of jumping in to define and solve the problem without taking the time to see the whole issue. I can be judgmental when I make decisions about what I think someone else should do and then think I have to be the one to make sure they do it.

In some ways, this is incredibly arrogant. I do know that my choices come from a place of genuine concern for those I love. My challenge is to sort out the distinction between what people want from me and what I can give. If I don't figure that out soon, like Humpty Dumpty, there will be no putting me back together again.

DANCING

Growing up, I knew Mom was in love with another man. Dad knew all about it; in fact he was in love with the same guy. Frank Sinatra. "Old Blue Eyes" was the guy, their favorite performer and they cherished the opportunity they had to hear him in concert. Not too long ago I was visiting and my parents were discussing how it was Frank's birthday, a date that is permanently etched in their minds. Frank's songs spoke to my parents much like a poet. For them, he put voice to their thoughts and feelings. For me, that man is Toby Keith. Anyone who knows me, understands I am nuts about the guy, a country singer of unusual talent. I have a car full of his CDs, even a fairly obscure Christmas one. I've seen him in concert on four occasions, and there is that memorable 2006 concert where Toby and I locked eyes from my seat in the 8th row. I'm convinced he remembers the moment with as much passion as I do. I sing with Toby in the car whenever I want to express a burst of energy. His lyrics hit every note on my emotional scale: joy, anticipation, sadness, regret, anger, and desire. Time and again, his music meets an unexpressed feeling or need, and I find myself getting lost in his songs. Despite my love for all things Toby, what really moves my soul is when I dance.

I am NOT a good dancer. I don't do much more than just shuffle my feet and swing my arms. The idea of line dancing makes me sweat since it involves way too much coordination and I've never been successful taking any kind of aerobics. But give me a space of carpet in the living room, some old time rock and roll and I can move! Julie couldn't contain her laughter when she found me this past weekend groovin' with our dog and Bob Seger, and I couldn't contain the urge to grab her hand and get her moving. Despite how much pressure is relieved when I dance, I don't do it nearly often enough.

A few months back I was out with my sister and some friends, listening to a band. As Barbie was kicking up a storm, I commented to a friend that I enjoyed watching my sister really let loose. He agreed and shared I could benefit from the same thing. I paused only briefly before hitting the dance floor and immediately felt a sense of release. It was one of those nights that didn't end until 3 a.m. and resulted in my sleeping through much of the next day. Boy, was it worth it! The joy, the exhilaration, and the unbridled freedom I felt while dancing was unbelievable! I find it almost impossible to feel worry or stress when I'm dancing and the sense of jubilation is like watching Snoopy gyrate to Schroeder's piano playing! Moving to music is so freeing, so full of energy, that I find it incredibly therapeutic. So the question again is, why don't I do the very thing that makes me so happy more often? Why, in the months since that night with my sister, have I not gone out dancing instead of renting a movie on a Saturday night?

Sadly, the answer is familiar: I continue to struggle with the sense that I'm not deserving of my own attention. Certainly, I do plenty of things I enjoy, but I rarely put myself before my job or family responsibilities. In my order of priorities, I most often put myself last. Yet, at other times, I see myself as incredibly selfish because I resent the demands that are placed on me. At those times, I don't feel as if I'm giving out of love but out of a sense of duty. That is in perfect keeping with the enabling part of my personality that consumes me! Somehow, I need to get off this hamster wheel that I find myself on and find time to dance. If I don't, I need to acknowledge I'm the one standing in the way.

There really is no reason that I can't dance more often. There are opportunities every day: I can dance in the living room, the kitchen, and even in the car. I can dance in the shower and when I am mowing the lawn. I can even dance in the rain; it's been done before! Most likely, Toby will be singing.

HOME

At the time Julie was born in South Dakota, my ex-husband and I were living in Carlisle, a small town in Pennsylvania. We were fortunate to live in a neighborhood where the neighbors really looked out for each other. While I was out west waiting for the paper work that would allow me to return east with infant Julie, our friends in Carlisle went to work. By the time we got back, the beginnings of a nursery were in place and we had everything we needed to get started. It was the kind of neighborhood where people helped each other shovel snow, rake leaves, and borrow sugar. During one particularly brutal April blizzard, I remember forcing our kids to trudge through the neighborhood delivering needed supplies. We adults stayed indoors keeping warm, laughing as we watched the kids pull on their boots for one more trip down the block! We traded babysitting services, killed mice when husbands were out of town, and drank each other's beer. A few of us regularly rose before dawn to walk the dogs and if a house was dark, we knew the previous night had been a late one and there was a woman down for the day. They were some of the happiest days of my life and on those early morning walks, I began the practice of identifying houses that were happy.

As the days here in Ohio begin to give way to slightly warmer temperatures, I've again begun to hit the pavement as part of my fitness routine. I've always loved walking and I'm trying to pick up the pace and do a bit of running. I'm trying to make a good hard walk part of my routine a few times a week, as both the dog and I need to shed a few pounds! It gives me a chance to again do one of my favorite things: look at houses. I taught Julie the art of assessing houses when she was quite young and by the time she was 10, she could spot one with good curb appeal. She would point out the details that would make a dwelling hard to sell, like a one car garage, overgrown shrubs, or peeling paint. She is drawn to extreme colors while I go for more subdued hues. Julie loves big dwellings; I prefer small, but we generally agree on which we think are happy.

There are certain clear criteria that tell me a house is content and, by association, the people who live there: a bit of color in the way of paint or accents, trimmed shrubs, and not in obvious need of repair. Any house that has either daffodils or tulips is automatically happy, as is one with chairs on a porch. I've determined that cheerful homes tend to be grouped together on a street, neatly arranged in a row. They shout out that they are more than houses; they are homes. Lately, I've been feeling a bit nostalgic for the sense of "home" I felt in Carlisle. Our house was definitely a happy one, and reflected a sense of comfort and acceptance that I haven't felt since.

By comparison, my house here does not meet any of my own criteria for being considered content. There is little color, no flowers, and nothing on the outside that draws folks in. It is a solid little place where Julie and I have lived since the divorce. My friends tell me that on the inside, there is a feeling of calm that was missing in the marital structure that Julie still refers to as "home", yet I feel something is missing.

I think that it's my unwillingness to accept where I am at this point. As I look back on the last year of sharing my rambling thoughts as a blogger (yes, it has been a whole year!), I realize that of all the queries I have raised, none is more central than this one: "Am I home"?

To answer that, I have to define what home means. Is it just where you live, or is it a state of being? Could it be the people you feel safe with or is it the space in which you can be yourself? Is home an acceptance of yourself regardless of the space you inhabit? Do we define our homes or do they define us? I don't have the answers, just the desire to make *this* house my home.

At the end of April, I will be returning to Carlisle for a visit. I plan to walk those familiar streets with old friends and check to see if my house is still happy. I plan to find the sense of peace I left there and bring it back to Cleveland. Then I'm going to plant colorful flowers, visit the ladies next door, and borrow some sugar. If a blizzard hits, I'll strap on my boots and see what my neighbors might need.

ROOTS

Last fall, in an effort to clear my garden of old growth, I dug up all the hosta plants. I'd been engaged in a three year battle for their souls with an army of slugs, and I decided to wave the white flag. I cleared the bed, all the while thinking how in the spring I'd have a new palette to design. Imagine my surprise in seeing tiny hosta leaves sprouting through the dirt! At first I thought that I'd not done a good enough job of digging them up. I'd dug down pretty deep and felt confident that I had removed them completely. But here they were, surviving despite my best efforts to the contrary.

My second thought was of my recent visit back to the old Carlisle neighborhood, and how roots run deep and spread far and wide. Mine are planted in more than one place: I feel drawn to the small town of Huron, OH because of my mother's history; I'm grounded in Cleveland because of my history, and I was transplanted to Carlisle to create history.

When I drove into that little Pennsylvania borough, I was surprised at how quickly I became emotional. Hundreds of memories flooded over me as I passed familiar places. The townhouse we rented when we first arrived in town, our favorite restaurant, the courthouse where we adopted Julie, even the grocery store, reminded me of the many happy years there. By the time I arrived at my friend Barbara's house, I was a mess. Within seconds of seeing her face, my heart began to sing with the joy of being home. I wasn't born in that little town, but it's where I first felt a sense of family among people to whom I wasn't related.

There have been many moments over the past few years that I've wondered what my life would be like if we hadn't moved away from Carlisle. Would my marriage have survived? What would Julie be like? Would I have grown professionally? Ridiculous questions, really, because they have no answers. Even though I have an incredibly strong faith that I'm exactly where I should be at this moment in time, the questions nagged at me. Visiting with dear friends, I couldn't help but reflect on how even those relationships would have been different and I found my emotions shifting all over the place. I was frustrated knowing, that since moving, I'd been physically unavailable to people when they struggled with life's hardships. I rejoiced at the spirit and accomplishments of young children who have grown into dynamic, interesting adults. I commiserated about aching joints, aging parents, and grieved when told of losses. With each shared memory, I felt the strength of the roots I'd put down and even saw a pink azalea I had planted years earlier in full bloom. As much as I took away from my nine years there, a huge part of me remains. I'm connected to that town, to those friends, to those memories in a permanent way. Our separate experiences have been grafted to one another and the new growth is indeed beautiful.

After a last few hugs and tears, I drove out of town with a tremendous sense of calm. For the first time in forever, I found myself making peace with all that has happened in the years since I left Carlisle. I don't need to hold on to hurt and pain any longer; I've spent enough time there. The next several hours found me driving back to my existing life with a freedom that was almost intoxicating.

This weekend, I studied those hostas and admired their determination. I removed all of the surrounding weeds, worked fresh top soil and fertilizer into the dirt, and bought slug bait. Then, in an act of pure optimism, I planted zinnia seeds. By summer, I will have an explosion of color in my yard that will remind me of my own growth over the last few years. Those tiny seeds will take root and grow with abandon. As will I.

PILLOWS

For many of my childhood years I shared a bed with my sister, Barbie. It was big and we were small, so there was plenty of space. Oh, there was the fairly regular battle for the covers but, for the most part, we slept peacefully side by side. That is until the night she fell asleep with gum in her mouth. That gum found its way to my pillow where it became attached to my neck and hair. I remember waking up unable to lift my head without the hairs on my neck being yanked out. I repeatedly found my way to my parent's room, complaining that something was wrong, but they kept sending me back to the sticky bed. By morning, that little piece of gum was so entangled in my hair and tattooed on my neck that Mom had to spend hours removing it with ice cubes and razor blades. I spent the next several days chomping Juicy Fruit in front of Barbie, who was not allowed to chew for a month! I also knew that I needed my own bunk.

It was years before Barbie and I got our own rooms. I cherished the freedom to spread out and not fight for space or blankets. I relished the feeling that my dreams were private. We traded bedrooms often throughout our high school years, but never again shared a bed. I didn't miss her. It was glorious. Eventually, as happens in the natural course of life, I did again share a mattress with someone for many years. At the beginning of my marriage, no bed was small enough; by the end, nothing was big enough. While the demise caused great sadness, I did again grow accustomed to sleeping alone and again rejoiced at the space and freedom.

As I ever so cautiously consider exploring new relationships, I wonder at my ability to share space and again accommodate someone else. I want to share time with someone; I'm just not sure I want to negotiate bathroom routines. Right now, one of the best feelings in the world is a cold pillow. Waking in the middle of the night with a hot flash and being able to roll over and find a cold spot is absolute heaven. I'm not sure I can give up that pleasure. Does having a relationship mean I have to? I don't know, since my perceptions of intimacy change with the weather.

The irony of this dilemma is not lost on me. A year ago, I was in a steady panic about Julie leaving and being alone with myself. Now I feel incredibly territorial about my space and prepare for her temporary return with a bit of dread. Julie being home for the summer will disrupt my new normal routine! I feel a tad annoyed that my comings and goings and my daily patterns will again have to be negotiated with someone else. I've joked with my friends that the perfect relationship would be with someone who lives a couple of hours away: close enough to get together for an event, but far enough that expectations don't become unrealistic.

A few weeks back, I actually had dinner with a man who was not married and not serving me a drink. I'm not sure it was a date, but I was nervous! I realized how much I miss having a male perspective in my world and I left the restaurant wanting to spend more time with him. Since I've become pretty independent I worry I've become too selfish to open my life. I know with some confidence that no one who enters my life now will ever know all the secrets I keep. On the plus side, I now choose not to share my past hurts and disappointments and to live in the moment. When I need to revisit my prior life, I can go to the people who lived through it with me. On the flip side, does that mean I will hesitate to let anyone in far enough to share my heart? I wonder whether I will ever again trust someone with those stories.

I worry that there will come those inevitable moments (losing someone I love), when all I have is the pillow. It's those nights, when I'm most vulnerable, that the cold pillow brings no relief. It won't matter that I am comfortable with being alone. It won't matter that I love my own space. It will only matter I feel an emptiness in my soul that only a live person can fill. At that moment I will simply miss being part of something bigger than myself. I will miss sharing the pillow.

Truth be told, I did miss Barbie when we got our own rooms. We may have quit sharing the same four walls, but we continued to share time, clothes, and make-up. We still fought over sister stuff and argued about whose turn it was to unload the dishwasher. We kept secrets and had the other's back when rules were broken. But I never again let her have any of my gum.

BEAUTY

On a recent road trip, my friend, Suzanne, and I were passing time by asking each other life questions. She asked me to remember a time I felt beautiful. My first thought was my wedding, before I recalled a trip to Florida when I was about 25. I was skinny, tan, and, in one photo, had a smile as big as the wide brimmed hat I was wearing. The picture is buried somewhere in the pile of photos under my bed, but the memory is clear. I felt beautiful. I can't say that particular feeling is common for me, and this weekend I was reminded that beauty comes in many forms.

The idea to do the Warrior Dash seemed like a good one. I would spend the winter months training by running on the treadmill, lifting weights, and strength training. I spent more time than I wanted on the elliptical, a machine that I despise. When the weather broke, I began to run sprints outside; I felt stronger but not ready. Running and I have never been friends. I've tried to embrace it as a form of exercise every decade of my adulthood and always come to the same conclusion: I hate it. Still, my friends convinced me the Warrior Dash was less about running and more about fun. The goal was not the time it took to get to the finish line, but just getting there! I knew some of the obstacles were going to significantly push me out of my comfort zone, and I was prepared to skip a few if necessary. My excitement grew about joining my friends in this madness before insecurities started to sink in.

The night before the event, Suzanne and I left the hotel to find a place to listen to music. We stumbled into a little bar where we found two women wearing the coveted "warrior" hats: fuzzy black with white horns. Thousands of racers were registered over two days, and they had completed the course just hours earlier. As we picked their brains for details, I began to feel unprepared. These women were quick to describe the event as easy, but they were toned and fit. There was no way I was ready!

Back in our room, I slept very little as I began to focus on my limitations. Once again, I was assuming that I would fail and was, in fact, only failing to see the possibilities. I awoke with a million rationalizations as to why I would be unable to participate. I popped a few Advil, ate a healthy breakfast of eggs and sausage, and attempted to re-adjust my thinking. Tough task!

The dash was held on acres of rural farm land and the temperatures were well into the 80's. Meeting the team members of our other insane friends, we registered and collected the timers to be attached to our shoe laces. Thousands of participants were set to do the run in staggered starts and several hours later, there I was standing in the queue waiting for the horn and feeling like I wanted to be anywhere but there. I felt old. I felt fat. I definitely did not feel beautiful. But then the music started and I was swept up in the crowd. There was no turning back without being trampled.

The run up the first hill quickly became a challenge. The serious athletes were in a full on run while the majority of us quickly found the incline too steep to jog. As we continued to work our way up the hill, the crowd thinned as people tried to find their own pacing and footing. A turn at the top led to an equally steep climb down, but in mud as far as the eye could see! The next half hour was a combination of climbing over logs in neck deep water, jumping over junk yard cars/tires, and crawling through a dark tunnel on my knees. Mostly it was a steady climb up and down hills of mud and more mud. At some point we all gave up trying to walk down the hills and just sat down, treating the muck as a slide. I knew these clothes would never make it home!

To that point, the challenges had been manageable. Then came the cargo net: a 20-foot wall of rope to climb. I quickly scanned the landscape for an escape and determined that there was no way out but up and over. I grabbed a rung, put my foot in another and began to work my way to the top.

I can't pinpoint the exact moment my feelings began to shift from fear to exhilaration. By the time I hit the ground on the other side of that net I was high on my own endorphins. I actually began to get excited about the next challenge and soon found myself running toward the climbing wall that I most feared. Standing at the bottom, I paused briefly before I grabbed the rope and actually scaled the side! Once over, I knew the final obstacles were at the end of a short river run, and I could hear the crowd cheering for the participants. When I rounded the bend and saw the fire and mud pits, I took off in a sprint. I leapt over the fire and didn't hesitate before landing in the mud and beginning the final crawl under barbed wire to the finish line.

There were my friends, covered in mud and smiling from ear to ear. We had all completed the course and looked like crap. But I don't think I've ever seen a more beautiful group of women. The confidence we all felt actually made each of us glow, despite looking like we had been dipped in milk chocolate. Several high fives and pictures later, we ventured to the fire hoses to be washed down. Still muddy, we needed to find a place to ditch our ruined shoes and change into dry clothes. The bathroom at the local KFC served the purpose, and only then did we put on our warrior hats and settle in for the trip home.

The lessons I need to learn in this life have always come in interesting forms. Who knew that the Warrior Dash would lead me to see that beauty may exist in the messiest of places. I will always have challenges and at times feel inadequate. When I do, I will think of that cargo net and that wall. I will look at the pictures of my friends covered in mud and see only their smiles. For years, my mantra to Julie has been "You are strong, you are smart, you are beautiful." This weekend I learned the same thing applies to me. I'm not 25, skinny, and tan. I am 55, average, and pale. Still, the smile in those muddy pictures equals that smile in the photo from Florida. The grin as I leapt over the fire pit is as wide as my new hat. And it looks damn good on me.

ELIZABETH

In the children's book *Paper Bag Princess*, Elizabeth is a beautiful princess engaged to marry the prince. A fierce dragon burns down her castle and carries off the prince, leaving Elizabeth with only a paper bag to wear. Elizabeth, intent on saving the prince, uses her superior intelligence to incapacitate the dragon and rescue her true love. The prince is less than grateful and he is horrified by her burned hair and dirty paper bag. Elizabeth, shocked by his lack of gratitude, literally skips out. They didn't get married. This book has been a gift to countless nieces and nephews, hoping they would get the moral of the story. I read it to Julie until she had it memorized.

I believe one of the things I've done best with Julie is to frequently remind her of her strengths and to empower her to trust her own abilities. I've always wanted her to be like Elizabeth and rely on her own instincts and wits. I hope over the past few years, when Julie and I have been on our own, I've role modeled those skills for her. Lately I find myself weary of slaying the everyday dragons of managing my own life.

The universe seems to be presenting me with everyday complications that take up a lot of energy and I find myself really missing, for the first time in quite a while, having someone who could share the load. The lawn mower broke. A mouse invaded my house. Julie's purse was stolen from the movie theater. Included in her bag was our garage opener and her driver's license. Whoever took the bag had our address and access to the house. We slept with lots of lights on that night and the next day was a blur of police reports, closing bank accounts, getting a replacement license, and phone calls. By noon, I was close to meltdown mode as I needed to learn how to reprogram the garage door and fix the mower before the rain started. All I kept thinking was that I wish a man was around to take care of it all. I sent out an SOS to no avail. Then, to add to the cluster, my car broke down while driving Julie back to school, three hours from home! It's actually still there while a new transmission is being built and installed.

The fact is that I'm surrounded by Elizabeths. The pictures of sisters, friends, and nieces cover my fridge and fill my living room. These capable gals have saved my ass more times than I can count. When I need help, I know I have multiple people to call, but it's the calling that has me feeling sad. It's in the calling that I've realized I'm no one's priority; I'm not first on anyone's list of concerns. A pang of sadness jabbed at my heart, while at the same time, I felt the earth tilt just a little bit as if to remind me that I needed to accept my reality.

I've never been one to pay attention to the obvious and find myself looking in all the wrong places to fill the void. As I gather the courage to enter the dating world, I seem to be attracted to men who are unavailable for one reason or another. Even when my gut tells me I need to accept my life as a single person, I have trouble accepting I'll always be the one shoveling the snow.

I want to spend time with a man. There, I said it. I want to be taken care of; I want to have someone else take the car for an oil change. I've proven I can handle all this stuff, I just don't want to anymore. I not only want to share the day-to-day life tasks, I want to share life experiences like cooking and movies and traveling. I want someone around to hold my hand and engage in the end of day chatter that comes with a relationship.

I fear I've spent too much emotional energy wishing a prince would just show up and fix the mower, trap the mice, and take care of the car. I fear he's not coming. The possibility exists that I may not again feel protected from life's storms. I need to figure out what that means to me and for me. I spent the last year adjusting to living by myself and taking care of everything. Most days, my confidence has grown. If I do open up enough to allow someone to share the load, how do I share my vulnerabilities without losing the strengths I've discovered? I need to figure out how to create balance.

In the meantime, I will continue to feel grateful for all the Elizabeths in my life, the women who are there to bolster me up when I feel less than capable. They are amazing in their ability to accomplish almost anything and are always available to help: the sister who disposed of the dead mouse, the friend who picked me up when my car broke down 200 miles from home, and the friend who loaned me a car until mine was fixed. I also can't forget the friend who threatens to smack me when I doubt my strengths. In those moments when I need help, I am their priority, and for that I am most grateful. Even if all I have is a paper bag.

LIGHTHOUSE

In New Orleans for a conference, I was startled to see a lighthouse. Since the city is bordered by water, it shouldn't have surprised me, but this one was landlocked in a retail district. Chuckling a bit, I wondered if the businesses had been built up around an actual lighthouse, or if maybe it was a replica. I chalked it up to being another interesting piece of the city. Back at home a few days later, I was walking with a friend near the lakeshore. A lighthouse I'd seen dozens of times before suddenly seemed larger and I couldn't avoid wondering if it had always been that big. The very next morning I opened the newspaper to find a half page picture of the same structure. I know that there have been times I've needed a 2' x 4' to the side of my head to get a message, but this had to be more than a coincidence. So what did it mean? Why did I need to think about lighthouses?

My first thought was of the solitary figure who works in that watchtower. My image is of a lone soul who keeps the lantern shining for stranded travelers, making sure the light is always visible. Those in trouble can see the beacon from miles away and know help is just over the next crest. Certainly that's similar to my role as a mother and was often my job as a wife. Right now I'm in danger of getting sucked into feeling responsible for the troubles of others. Julie is struggling with finding her path and her father is back in town fighting his own demons.

Each has a history of looking to me to fix the problems that their choices create. They seek my help in directing them to shore, in keeping them grounded. From my perch in the lighthouse, I can see where they should steer but I need to let them take whatever course they choose. Their individual journeys are their own and for Julie the most I can do is keep the light on; I can't make her follow it. For sure, I can't be the one to keep it shining for her father. Since I've been feeling the weight of handling issues on my own, maybe the lighthouses were here to remind me that I'm strong enough to continue to man the shore. Maybe it's a reminder that even when the waves are crashing against the rocks, the lighthouse is stable enough to bear the weight.

My next thought was to consider that I'm not the lighthouse but actually the one on the water. Was I being reminded that even when I'm feeling lost, even when I think I can't find my way, I can look toward something besides myself for guidance? I had a flashback to the weekend my car broke down. A new friend was incredibly generous in sharing his time and home to get Jules moved into her dorm, gave me a place to stay and a ride to where another friend could pick me up. At one point, I remember muttering to him that I hated not being in control. He quietly responded: "Maybe that's the problem". I was startled by his accurate observation and troubled that perhaps my confidant facade was not as clever as I'd assumed. I have great caring friends and family; perhaps I need to let myself rely on their guidance more often, and quit feeling I need to do it all.

One more possibility came to mind. Maybe, just maybe, the lighthouses are here to tell me not to give up hope. There's no question that I'm surrounded by the struggles of those I love. I'm also surrounded by faith and optimism; perhaps I've fallen, again, into the habit of not noticing. I took a moment to reflect on what signs of hope are casting a light on my life. There's the niece who texts to say my sense of adventure is an inspiration to her. Parents at school send me thank you notes for simply doing my job. Julie, sharing her small triumphs along with her struggles, is a bright beam. My dad, who fights his body every day and Mom who cares for him, are constant reminders of determination and commitment. I have a friend and brother who have both beaten cancer and another who has survived it twice. My young niece and nephew who jump up in excitement when they see me, eager to welcome me into their world, promise to keep me young. I have the opportunity to greet every day with the idea that love is possible.

These are my lanterns; these are the beacons guiding me to shore. The lighthouses have simply been popping up to make sure that I see them.

MIKE

When my mother died, I never saw it coming. I wasn't scared by the prospect of losing her because I didn't have a frame of reference for the magnitude of such a tremendous loss. Frustrated by the limited images I can recall, I've spent countless years of my life trying to remember even the smallest details. Periodically I would be told a story by a cousin or other relative that would add to the information, but not to the memories. There is a hole in my heart that's never been filled, and it will soon be bigger. This time I do see it coming. This time I'm scared to death.

My father is dying. His struggle with Parkinson's is becoming more than he can win. The family has been told that he will most likely lose this fight in the next three months. Ninety days. I have plenty of memories of my father: I remember holidays, birthdays, and weddings; I remember tender moments and fights. There are times I'm sure we disappointed each other and there are moments we shared that no one else knows. Memories are not the problem. The problem is not knowing how to spend this time with my dad. How do I learn the things I don't know about him? What are the things I don't know? What will I regret not asking? Basically, how do I prepare for a life that will not have him in it? I don't have a clue.

For years, I've spent part of each weekend visiting Dad. I have to admit there were times I didn't want to go, it felt inconvenient. More often I did; I wanted to spend even an hour catching up, playing cards, watching a ball game. I know he was particularly happy when I brought him cookies or apple pie (I do, after all, come by my sweet tooth honestly). Often I left wondering how I'd feel if that visit would be the last time I saw him. Would I feel that the time spent had been enough? Would I feel that I'd said all I wanted or needed to say? Never did I leave without saying "I love you", knowing those are the last words I want him to hear from me. Yet each time, I never really believed it was the last time. There was always next weekend, always another opportunity. Now what?

Does the knowledge that the inevitable is actually coming change how I spend time with my dad? Does it change how long or how often I visit? Does it mean that I drop by every day for a few moments, or stay longer on fewer days? Does it mean that I put my life on hold to prepare, or do I live so that I am prepared?

Am I sad each time I see him or allow myself to laugh? Again, I don't have a clue.

Here's what I do know: I'm not going to get any answers. I'm rightfully in uncharted waters, and for the next three months I'll be treading like crazy. If there's ever been a time that I needed to live in the present moment, this is it. I need to wake each day with no expectations and grateful that I will have one more opportunity to tell my dad that I love him. I'm going to take the advice of my young niece, Madeline. She told me that everyone hates the day they get this news and that I should try to see him as much as I can before "it" happens. This time belongs to him; whatever words he has yet to say, whatever wisdom he has yet to impart, it's my job to listen.

I have a lot to do in these next few months. I want to make sure I don't forget one thing about Dad. I'm going to hold his hand and kiss his cheek. We're going to play gin, and I'm going to make all the foods he's not allowed to have. I'm going to sit by his side for as long as he wants, and I'm going to write about him. Telling the stories of my dad will cement these remaining days to the years of stored memories. Join me on this journey. Let me tell you about my dad, Mike. Let me tell you the things I want to remember.

DECISION

Back in the mid-70's, Dad was not a feminist. Even though years later I came to know him as very open-minded and proud of my accomplishments, he didn't encourage me to go to college. Instead, Dad told me that nursing would be a good career for a "girl" and instructed me to apply to the local hospital program. Excited to be pleasing him, I sat for a chemistry exam as part of the evaluation process. A few weeks later, I received my acceptance letter with the stipulation that I take a summer chemistry class. I withdrew my application.

Not sure what I might want to do, I enrolled at the local university for a year before stupidly following my boyfriend to his school on the other side of the state. Again, my father shook his head and warned me that the decision was short-sighted. Desperate to set my own destiny, I committed to my coursework in home economics and graduated with honors...with no job skills! I did get a job that eventually led to another, that led to graduate school to study social work. Life provided me with opportunities that lit my path, and I've never once regretted following my instincts. But Dad was right about one thing: the boyfriend thing did not work out.

For Dad and me, there was no discussion about my future...he knew best until that day I was assertive enough to disagree. He was smart enough to let me figure it out on my own, and I was able to prove him wrong. All these years later, in my role as a guidance counselor, I often observe the disconnect between what students feel and parents think. It's a delicate balance families negotiate when making decisions about college. Generally, I ask students to respect the wisdom of their parents and for parents to trust the instincts of their daughters.

When the time came for Julie to decide, I needed to follow my own advice. Yes, I wanted Julie to attend a small college, but she was intent on the large university. I worried from the first day that she wouldn't manage the experience. She attended a small private high school where teachers are greatly committed to the success of their students. In choosing a large school, Julie was sure that she would be able to seek help when needed, structure study time, and work independently. I was doubtful, as these were skills she was still developing! Just as Dad had allowed me, I needed to let Julie figure it out.

It turns out I was right. I chalked the first quarter difficulties up to adjustment issues, the second to roommate problems, and the third to a lack of advising. When her grades were marginal at the end of her first year, I struggled with whether I would allow Julie to return. But she spent the summer evaluating her direction and recommitting to the process. Jointly, we set goals and decided to give it one more shot. My desire for her success provided enough denial to ignore my instincts.

I should have taken my car breaking down as a sign. Thirty minutes outside campus, my transmission died. After getting the car, stuffed with clothes and supplies, towed to a local dealer, I called on a local friend/colleague to help get Julie moved into the dorm. He gave me a place to stay, and the next day, drove me two hours to meet a friend to get me home. Six weeks later, when I went to get her for a weekend visit, my car broke down in the same spot...again the transmission. I figured I better start paying attention to these scowls from the universe.

When I paused, and did, I could see Julie struggling with the news of my dad's worsening illness. They shared a special bond and a certain part of her family identity was tied to her grandfather. Our conversations were increasingly about what was going wrong with school, rather than what was going right. Distracted, her motivation was waning, and all those good intentions from the summer were fading. I could hear the desperation in her voice but also the anger at herself. As much as I needed to back off, to let Julie own the process, I knew that a decision needed to be made, and I would be the one to make it. As the quarter came to an end, there was no denying it...she needed to come home. Neither one of us was prepared to continue to invest our money and energies.

These are the moments that make parenting tough. Breaking curfew or getting caught smoking, are easy problems to address compared to watching our kids make choices that alter the course of their lives. Grounding our children for skipping school or being disrespectful generally teaches a lesson that, hopefully, they only need to learn once. Other lessons seem to take longer to sink in, and so the consequences may be more difficult, more serious. I could so clearly see her not using her abilities and gifts, yet there was no other alternative. Julie needed a new path and time to find it. My job had to be more supportive than directive, and I needed to bite my tongue A LOT! Now was not the time for criticism or "I told you so."

Going off to college was supposed to be the natural next step; coming home was not. Packing Julie up was far more painful than settling her in a little over a year ago. There was no excitement or optimism to balance out the worry. Julie felt defeated, embarrassed. If I were honest, I felt frustrated and irritated. The ride home was somber, heavy with disappointment and resignation. The sun was shining, but it was not visible through the cloud of regret that followed us north. I attempted to lighten the mood by suggesting a series of car games, anything to switch the focus. But just as she had 18 months earlier, Julie responded by again plugging in her iPod and sitting back.

Despite all my angst about living alone, I'd grown accustomed to not sharing the bathroom. There are no dirty dishes in the sink when I get home from work and no wet towels left in the washing machine. I fall asleep without wondering when she gets home and there is always enough milk in the fridge. In some ways, I'm going to need to make psychological space in both my head and the house, and together we will figure out a new balance.

That challenge will be complicated by Dad's declining health. Julie and I are each off kilter as Thanksgiving is just days away and we know it will be Dad's last, followed by his last Christmas. This will be Julie's first loss, the first funeral of someone she adores. Facing that pain, in the face of her own self-doubts will be a double hit. Not knowing exactly when it's coming makes looking forward particularly tough. For both of us.

When I changed my mind about nursing school, Dad wasn't happy. I can appreciate his worry, concerned that I was making a bad decision. He thought he had me all figured out and that he was pointing me in the right direction. I'm sure at the time he was frustrated that I wasn't appreciating his wisdom, not seeing the bigger picture. The truth is, I was. It's just that it was different than what he saw.

I don't have a clue what the next step is for Julie. Just as my father did for me 40 years ago, I need to let her figure that out. I'm pretty sure she will.

WALLPAPER

Growing up, I don't ever recall my parents hiring people to do work at our house. With six kids, there was no need for outside help with cleaning or yard work. I've raked more leaves out of pachysandra than I care to remember and Julie still complains about how my cleaning borders on obsessive. If something was broken, my dad fixed it. If something needed to be built, he did it. He laid carpet, painted walls, and fixed plenty of backed up toilets. Still, nothing got his juices flowing like wallpapering a room.

My memory is that as soon as one room was completed, it was time to move on to the next. Once they were all done, it was time to start over. When grasscloth paper became popular, there was a new passion. Every room and the inside of some cabinets were papered with this textured stuff and he even used it to cover our school books! More than one Christmas present wound up being wrapped in leftover scraps and patching was easy because rolls of paper were stored in the basement. Because it was a project evening, there's the memorable photograph of Dad in his tattered khakis and paint stained sweatshirt standing next to my date and me prior to a winter formal! Because he was good at it, Dad was also often invited to help wallpaper the homes of friends and relatives. Everyone once in a while, he would call on me to help him and I would, of course, aggravate him.

The problem was that I could never "see" what he saw. I had no clue how to measure the wall or where to start. It always amazed me that he would look at a room and figure out in which corner to start; in my mind, just pick a spot and get going. I didn't understand what "drop" or "match" meant, wallpapering terms that are branded on my subconscious, but that I still don't get! The words "measure twice, cut once" meant I was stuck there for longer than I wanted. I didn't understand why you had to prep the pieces, or the wall; just stick the damn stuff up and let's go! To me, the goal was to use the paper to cover up a flaw. What did it matter what you did to the wall first? I remember one particularly painful Sunday afternoon that he was actually papering the kitchen ceiling! He had me on the ladder holding strips in place so he could cut the next one. Naturally, they would shift, and he'd have to take it down and start over. Let's just say that my own knowledge of foul language was greatly enhanced that day!

One would think that with all that papering going on, I would've picked up some level of skill but, NO! When my own first home was in need of some updating, Dad came for a weekend and we did three rooms in less than two days. I watched, slapped on paste, and handed him tools like a nurse assists a surgeon. He was methodical and precise, barely stopping for food or drink. I kept looking for the genetic link...why didn't I understand this? Was it my lack of math skills or inability to cut a straight line? Or perhaps, as my older brother and sister often teased, I actually WAS adopted! Over the years I've wondered what I might have learned from watching my dad and enduring the hours of helping him. Maybe it had nothing to do with hanging paper on a wall. Maybe I took what I observed and stored it in my psyche in a different way.

When my father surveyed a room to figure out where to start, he was actually solving a puzzle. How were all the pieces going to fit together? When he prepped the wall and the paper, he was actually fixing the underlying problem so that when the paper was hung, it would stay. Dad was a master at wallpaper because he did it right. He didn't hang it to hide flaws, but to enhance the room, the house. It's sort of like what I do as a counselor. I help folks look at the rooms of their lives, patch the holes, and accept the flaws.

As I have struggled this week with the news of Dad's impending death, I realize that I've become a master at covering up my own flaws. Someone recently told me I was quite sophisticated in articulating my BS. I talk a good game but have trouble accepting that I can't always handle everything perfectly. This same someone suggested that I just may need to peel back some of the paper and look at what's underneath. Damn. What corner do I actually start in? How can I do it without the teacher?

Although my father hasn't wallpapered a room in many years, I do remember the basics of what he taught me. Have the right tools and don't rush. Look at the whole room and start with one piece at a time. Fix what's underneath. I can almost hear him say: "Do it right the first time." If I do, perhaps I will finally see what he saw.

MOMENTS

A couple of years ago on one of my Sunday visits with Dad, we were discussing the funeral of a friend. Dad was in a particularly reflective mood, needing to talk about the kind of service he wanted. We talked about music, we talked about the church, and we talked about the wake. It was at this point, despite the serious nature of the conversation, we got a little crazy. The plan was simple: Dad would record comments to greet folks as they approached the casket. I would control them from the other side of the room. Old friends would hear, "It's about time you came to see me." Others would hear, "How do I look?" Dad's children would each hear: "You were always my favorite." He and I laughed to the point of tears and Mom just sat staring as if we were crazy. Dad made it clear that when the time came, he wanted to hear his family laugh, to celebrate his life. When I kissed him good bye on that Sunday, I was grateful for any time I could spend with him and remembered to once again say "I love you."

Today I kissed my father good bye for the last time. Those "90 days" we were given by the doctor turned into only 14 and Dad passed away this afternoon. He'd been negotiating with God for the last several days and, after spending a moment alone with each of us today, Dad quietly moved on. The images of the past week are exploding in my brain as I try to make sense of the hole in my heart that will never be repaired.

I knew on Sunday. I sat holding Dad's hand and I could feel his weariness, his willingness to let go. The quiet was both a welcome relief and a painful reminder of all that may be left unsaid. As I waited for Mom to come and spend the night at the nursing home, I fixed his blankets and put ice chips on his lips. I traced his fingers with my own, determined to remember the shape and feel. I quietly sang to him, "Fingerprints of God", a love song, and I gently kissed his eye lids. I knew.

Walking to my car I called Nancy and simply said: "You need to get here. It's time." For the next three days and nights, Dad's children took turns sitting with him. We loaded his room with family photos and played Sinatra and Streisand. There were equal amounts of tears and laughter as we watched and waited, knowing that this time, there would be no recovery, no "one more" trip home. Whatever time was left was going to be in this room. The moments passed slowly, each one hanging in the air to grab.

At dinner each night, the six of us told stories and wondered aloud what life would be like without Dad. It had been years since we shared this much time together as siblings and I couldn't help but think how happy that would make Dad. We discussed the funeral and found ways to distract our thinking. There was a nervous energy to our conversations, an uncomfortable sense of anticipation. It was as if we were all collectively holding our breath, and if one of us exhaled, we would—each one of us—collapse.

This morning, I awoke with an exhaustion I've never before experienced. From the moment my feet touched the floor, I felt the weight of the day. My head hoped for an end to his pain while my heart knew mine was just beginning. How could so many feelings be operating at the same time? How could I navigate through them all? I would never find out, as within hours, only one emotion remained: emptiness.

Despite being surrounded by people who love me, I've never felt more alone. After one last meal together, we scattered in different directions to grieve in private. It was the moment I had dreaded most for the past five years. Even though I have more than one friend who volunteered to spend the night, there is no comfort to be found. Dad is gone and the regrets are already floating on the edge of my consciousness. Did I spend enough time with him? Was I a good daughter? Why didn't we ever play golf?

It's not these questions that will haunt my sleep tonight, it's knowing that in the morning, it will still hurt. I will awake to a day that does not include my father and it's impossible to know how to move through that kind of world. Nothing I do tomorrow will make sense and nothing I do will lessen my pain.

We will meet with the funeral home, florist, and priest. We will plan the service to celebrate Dad's life and we will sort through pictures and memories to tell his story. I will write his eulogy and I will weep. I'll try to remember that Dad embraced his life fully and wanted us to laugh. I'll look for him everywhere and long to hear his voice.

When I get overwhelmed I'll remember those quiet moments last Sunday and remember all the Sundays we shared. I will allow my tears to flow and my heart to ache. I know that it's in that same broken heart that Dad will forever reside. I just need to sit quietly and feel him there. Every moment.

TRADITION

Growing up, Christmas was a pretty average affair. There were Easy Bake Ovens and bicycles, robes and socks, and of course, stockings full of candy. There were gift exchanges with aunts and uncles, my grandmother's Santa Claus cookies with coconut beards, and poking through closets looking for presents. Fairly standard holiday rituals, but there are a few special Christmas memories that do stand out.

It's hard to forget the year I was convinced I saw Santa fly over my grandparents' home, or the year we all drove down to Cleveland Public Square, which was magical with colored lights reflecting off the snow. We had dinner at Higbees, the local department store, and our spaghetti was served to us in little cardboard ovens. We hurried through the meal so we would not miss the opportunity to visit with Mr. Jing-a-Ling, Cleveland's version of a large, living elf. The night ended with buying presents at the Twigbee Shop, where kids could buy cheap, unnecessary gifts for their families. It was a scene right out of "A Christmas Story". Despite these stand-out memories, I don't recall specific traditions.

As we became adults and started to scatter around the country, it seemed harder to get everyone together. Marriages made gathering all of us all in the same room even more difficult, as we tried to balance our Christmas visits with the expectations of in-laws. My parents then made a simple request: "Share Christmas Eve with us". It was a great arrangement. Our family was all together on the 24th and free to meet the demands of others on the 25th. No one expected it to become the grand event of the year and a cherished memory for our kids.

But what a grand event it was! It meant good china and silver, candles and lace tablecloths, turkey dinner and those presents wrapped in wall paper! Dinner was a dress up occasion with the men in suits and ties, the ladies in fancy dresses. Dad wore his tuxedo with a bright red bow tie and looked every bit the sophisticated gentleman, holding court in his place at the head of the table. When the family grew, we added chairs and plank boards to make sure everyone was at one table. If someone couldn't get in from out of town, we did feel their absence, but the night didn't pass without talking to them on the phone. I remember the year my nephew Michael, only an infant, was dressed in a tux and red bow tie to match his grandfather. A tradition was born.

When my folks downsized to a smaller home, the celebration shifted to fit the space. No longer could we all sit around one table, but we could still fit in the house and still get dressed up. And Dad still wore his tux. We began to exchange fewer gifts, focusing on the presents for the little ones. The joy was in being together, with the grandkids running around, eager to open gifts and eat chocolate Rudolph lollipops. We returned to our individual homes with young ones who were ready to go right to bed with visions of Santa waiting to land on the roof.

The grand event began to rotate to different homes as Dad's health began to fail. Each year, the celebration belonged to someone else but remained a priority in the holiday planning. The last few years, the party became a much more casual affair and it became too much for Dad to manage the tuxedo. Dinner became buffet style and the gift exchange became a "white elephant". We added people to the party and lost a few. Although each year we silently wondered whether it would be Dad's last, we never really thought it was possible. Now we know it is.

The family gathered a lot over the last few weeks and shared more meals than we usually do in a year. Sharing countless stories and photographs, we've learned that what binds us together as a family has little to do with genetics. We are bound by memories, anchored by love; the love of a father we have only begun to mourn. Celebrating the grandest of events without the family patriarch seems nearly impossible to consider. Christmas Eve was about Dad being at the head of the table. It was about Dad pouring the wine. It was about Dad saying grace. There is no filling that chair.

This year, the first without Dad, we've decided to honor him with a return to tradition. The good china is coming out, the tablecloths being pressed. I'll continue the baking of dozens of Christmas cookies and Barbie will make Dad's favorite cheesy potatoes. The "white elephants" will be wrapped up in beautiful paper with magnificent bows to disguise what is inside. The ladies will again be in party dresses, the men in suits and ties. As the reluctant new patriarch, my brother Bob, will don the tux. A toast will be raised and a wish balloon released to the heavens as we smile through our tears.

Christmas morning, Dad loved to watch his brood rip open the packages. I can remember him sitting in his black leather wing back chair with a cup of coffee, waiting for the madness to end. I know this year Dad will again be watching it all but from his new place of honor, from inside our hearts. A very fine tradition.

PLUNGE

The idea came after the Warrior Dash. What would be the next challenge? I casually mentioned to Patty that it would be a kick to do the "Polar Bear Plunge." You know what I'm talking about.....insane people who run into Lake Erie, or another frigid body of water, on New Year's Day. I was surprised by her immediate commitment and the number of other friends who quickly agreed. When the senior member of our group nodded her intent to participate, I knew I was in trouble. Over the next six months it was talked about periodically, and everyone continued to commit. Others heard and signed on. Really? I'd watched videos of people doing the plunge in previous years and the doubts began creeping in. I wear sweats and socks to bed in the winter…what was I thinking?

As we gathered for our annual Christmas lunch, the friends began to formalize the plan. The "official" plunge takes place on New Year's Day and involves the signing of waivers, check-ins and hundreds of people. There were a few scheduling conflicts and the idea seemed on the verge of falling apart. But, as is often the case with this particular group of women, a new plan was hatched. Why not our own, private, plunge? New Year's Eve, mid-morning, local beach. All in. I waited, thinking someone was going to begin talking reason. I quietly mentioned that someone might want to exercise some common sense. Not a one. In fact, I was reminded that it was my idea.

The Plunge WAS my idea. I've often thought of doing it, yet here I was looking for an out. I realized that fear is my mantra, my defense mechanism. I can think of a million reasons not to take a risk, to play it safe, while admiring others who approach everything with a sense of adventure. I ultimately do what I set out to do, torturing myself mentally before I take the first step.

The past year certainly had its challenges. I've found myself in unfamiliar territory more often than not and my worst demons were faced. I survived taking Jules to meet her birth family, rode my bike 100 miles in one day, watched people I love experience hurt and betrayal, and buried my father. I entered and lost a writing contest (again) and actually explored dating. These experiences continued to present me with opportunities to ask myself questions designed to provide insight into this crazy life, and I continued to be my own worst enemy. Never was that more clear than during the last 24 hours, and I woke up this morning with a long list of reasons why the Plunge was a bad idea. Standing in a friend's living room, Patty simply looked at me and said: "Then don't do it." I realized if I just watched, I would forever regret the decision and I'd be no closer to really changing my own resistant mentality. So I headed to the beach with the others, realizing that *thinking* was not what was needed at the moment.

We stood in the parking lot wrapped in robes, jumping up and down. Pictures were taken, and we spoke of using the Plunge as a way to wash away all we hoped to leave behind from 2011. One friend demonstrated this by writing a list of her struggles in magic marker on her hand. There was the collective last minute hesitation as we stared at the chilly tide, until the first brave soul started down the steps to the water's edge.

Once on the sand, we took off multiple layers and faced the waves. The only rule was that you had to dip in far enough that your shoulders were wet. Holding hands in solidarity and screaming like little girls, we all ran in, sat down and got the hell out. In less than sixty seconds we were back on the sand, running for our towels. In another sixty seconds we were wrapped up and in our cars. We didn't need to say anything more to each other; our words had been left at the shore. The only goal at that point was to get home and into a very hot shower. In those frozen two minutes, I realized that 2011 was indeed over. I'd survived one more round of loss and came away cleansed.

A new year begins in just a few hours. 2012 does not arrive without complications. Jules is back living at home and I'm certainly not done grieving. I'm planning to greet this new year with the idea that the challenges I'm given are not there to slow me down but to keep me moving. I plan to remember every day that I'm blessed with new possibilities for growth. I hope to learn from each experience and I plan to say yes more than I say no.

Later this evening, as I share a Chinese dinner with a couple of other "plungers", I will raise a glass of champagne to all that I conquered last year and welcome all the adventures that await me. We will re-live the cold moments and pat ourselves on the back for being stupid. We will toast our bravery and our sense of adventure. We will share our resolutions and read our fortunes. Then I'll head home and shudder at the cold morning memory, even as I snuggle under an electric blanket.

THURSDAY

For most people, the Holy Trinity is represented by the Father, Son, and Holy Ghost. For me though, the Trinity is comprised of those three guardian angels: Virginia, Clara, and Winnie. Their presence and protection has been constant, while with my dad, all I feel is that he is gone. I don't doubt that he is cavorting with the Trinity, but I have yet to feel like he is watching. I've been looking for some sign that he is with me and until today, was missing the obvious. You see, today is Thursday.

Most days I wake up and before my feet hit the floor, I think about Dad. I have a brief conversation with him and God while I wrap my head around the fact that I can no longer see Dad's face. This is particularly true on Thursdays since that is the day he passed. It was also the day of the week I received my share of his ashes, and when I finally put away his eulogy, obituary, and prayer cards. I tend to feel the loss intensely on this day, wanting to talk about him so that his memory doesn't fade. Complicating it all is the knowledge that my mother also passed away on a Thursday. I have concluded that grieving over someone you know for a lifetime IS harder than grieving over someone who was taken way too early. I'm surprised by how often the tears come and how often my stomach hurts.

This morning started with driving to work while listening to Rod Stewart. I thought about Dad during morning prayer and again when a colleague asked about the holidays. As each hour passed, I found myself increasingly restless, a nagging, undefined thought floating on the edges of my consciousness. The more I tried to articulate the feeling, the more I felt it slipping through my thoughts. What was it about today, about this particular Thursday? The sense that I was supposed to understand something was overwhelming and I drove home in tears, frustrated by my inability to sort it out.

Myron Henry Emmerich was born on May 9, 1929. On that day, there was no sadness. As one of the first set of twins born in Vermilion, OH in over 50 years, his birth was a day of joy for my grandparents. Dad often joked that he was born at home because "I wanted to be close to my mother". Born during the Great Depression, Dad would say he never really felt deprived. His adolescence was full of friends, sports, girls, and weekends at the beach. As an adult, he was a pilot, a boater, a golfer, and a skier. Rarely did he tolerate sustained emotion, although as he aged he became much more expressive. He loved taking chances but also relished the safety of his home. Fiercely competitive, Dad loved to debate politics and many conversations with him ended in a draw. I don't remember one day when this man was not fully engaged in his life. Even when Dad was at his lowest, he was still looking forward.

Today Dad decided to let me know it was okay for ME to keep moving forward. It was Dad who prompted me to come home and sit down at the computer. It was Dad who prompted me to "google" his birthday. It was Dad who calmed my heart when it popped up that he was actually born on a Thursday! I instantly realized he doesn't want it to be dedicated to grieving; he wants me to dedicate Thursdays to living. Yes, Dad wants me to remember, but he wants me to remember his life not his death.

I miss Dad more than I can say. I miss him every moment of every day. What I miss most is his spirit. Today he let me know that he is indeed with me, watching. Along with the Holy Trinity, he wants me to embrace this life, to live every moment. Especially on Thursdays.

CARDS

Over the span of 56 years, I've played countless games of cards. As kids, my sister Barbie and I played Concentration, Rummy, War, and an interesting painful little game known as Bloody Knuckles. I don't remember the exact rules but I do remember that the loser had to endure the scraping of her knuckles with a handful of cards. It hurt! In college I learned Spades and Crazy Eights, and Julie developed a love of Uno. I think Euchre, my favorite game, is a simple man's bridge. It might surprise some people, and others not at all, that I am a tad bit competitive. This trait, which I did inherit from Dad, has me always ready for a friendly game.

As Dad grew less and less mobile, his desire to play cards grew. A weekly poker game at the community center provided him with social contact, competition, and sometimes a few extra bucks. He had a friend who would visit regularly to play gin, and it was our game of choice on many Sunday afternoons. Cards provided us both with a distraction from the obvious…his increasing struggle with his body, his losing battle with Parkinson's. A game with Dad almost always involved a discussion of strategy, mutual criticism of each other's play and whatever cookies I'd baked him that week. If he was having a good day, Dad could take his turn at dealing but as his disease progressed, shuffling became my job.

Whenever Dad was in either the hospital or rehab, I always took a deck of cards for a visit, and one Saturday night, we had a marathon gin game before the nursing staff suggested I leave. We were well matched. I beat him as often as I was beaten, and we periodically accused each other of cheating. I was always startled at how he could manage scoring three games simultaneously and never be wrong on the math. Then there were the afternoons when I believed he was falling asleep and he would, with eyes half-closed, call "Gin". I learned, never count him out.

As I adjust to a world that does not include my dad, I struggle with wondering if he now knows that sometimes I didn't want to play. From where he now sits, can he see that sometimes I was frustrated when playing? Does he now know that sometimes I chose to play cards because I had nothing else to say? Is he aware that I felt some annoyance when he dropped his cards? In other words, has he found all the things that I keep hidden from everyone? I worry that if he can, he is deeply disappointed.

I did plenty of things to make my dad proud. He appreciated my visits and looked forward to whatever time I spent with him. He probably knew there were days I visited out of a sense of duty and obligation, even while knowing my visits were based in love and respect. I regret those times with Dad that I felt impatient, and I wish I had those moments back. It makes me reflect on how I balance what I think and feel with how I act. Am I living my life in a way that mirrors my values? Am I making decisions that are in keeping with the kind of person I strive to be? If Dad is now in a place from which he can see it all, am I okay with that?

For the most part, the answer is yes. I live my values and make choices that are in sync with my beliefs. I treat others with respect and choose not to have judgmental people in my inner circle. When I'm honest, there are those occasions when I behave in ways I criticize in others. Sometimes, I'm the only one who knows when that happens and I chastise myself. I mean I know we're meant to have flaws; I know we are designed as imperfect. So why do I worry that my dad, or anyone for that matter, knows what those flaws are?

Because I think we're also designed to want to be better. I choose to believe that most of us actively work to overcome our weaknesses and develop our gifts. We are never going to meet everyone else's expectations, and God only knows we will probably never live up to our own. But I, for one, will continue to try, continue to be the person I envision.

I haven't played gin since Dad died. For some reason it just doesn't seem right to play with anyone but him. That doesn't change my love of playing cards. Tonight I'm going to play Euchre with girlfriends. Not exactly cigars and scotch, more like wine and hummus. I will good-naturedly accuse my opponents of cheating, criticize their play, and question my partner's strategy. I imagine Dad will be watching and may even try to slap the cards out of my hand when I play the wrong one. I'll imagine him sneaking a cookie from the table and taking his turn dealing. I'll allow myself to feel his presence and will know that even with him gone, I should still never count him out.

YARN

There is something uniquely special about a yarn shop. Entering is a bit like finding yourself on the other side of the rainbow, as your senses are hit with an explosion of color and textures. Looking at all the options can keep me hooked for hours as I consider all the possibilities. With winter having finally arrived, I recently went looking for a new project, something I could finish just in time for spring sweater season. I finally settled on a pattern and a lovely cotton taupe yarn, and headed home to curl up and get started.

The problems started when I couldn't find the beginning strand. The yarn had not come in a traditional skein; it was something I later learned was called a "hank". It looked a bit like a figure 8 and needed to be untwisted. I found a corner where it was tied and, of course, I gave it a good snip. I had an end and I began to pull so I could wind the strands into a ball. As I pulled, the yarn immediately began to get tangled. I paused to try and locate the problem but felt like the best answer was to continue to pull. The harder I pulled, the more tangled the soft string became until, all too soon, I had a mass of spun cotton that would never be part of a sweater. In disgust, I put it on a table and picked up a new hank. Having learned my lesson, I discovered how to create a round of twisted strands without creating a ball of knots. I didn't start my project on that evening.

The next morning, tea cup in hand, I found myself staring at the knotted clump. My first thought was to pitch it and just replace the whole thing. My time was certainly worth more than seven bucks, and the task of untangling the yarn seemed daunting. But it was cold and wet outside, a good day to stay in my pajamas and solve a puzzle. I got comfortable, picked up the mess and got started.

I'm not sure the exact moment I realized that the collection of knots was a metaphor for the state of my heart. Since the death of my dad, I have found my emotions to be as tangled as this lovely taupe string. This loss has set into motion a host of feelings and thoughts that are tied together in complicated patterns of love and sadness. The loss of my marriage had already created a hole in my heart and my father's death has made that hole bigger. It's time to untangle the mess so that my heart can open up to new experiences.

Six hours. It took four episodes of "Law and Order" and a Lifetime movie to untangle that mess. I found a delicate balance between following the string, opening up holes and rewinding the freed strands into a ball. I had to continue to work over and under the maze of yarn, sometimes freeing several inches at a time, and sometimes having to stop and locate where the roadblock originated. I kept thinking that at any moment, I would reach the point where everything would loosen up and there would be no more snags or tangles. As I reached the end, I found the source: one very small knot that had set everything else in motion. This is where my heart is stuck.

I don't think that I've ever completely recovered from the betrayal of my marriage. The damage that was caused is hindering my ability to see what other options this life might have in store for me because I remain too tied to the past. No doubt I've moved forward, found new friendships, and discovered my adventurous side. Julie and I are solid in our relationship and I'm comfortable in my own skin. But the knot of betrayal leaves me feeling unworthy and cautious in my ability to trust, which my grief has forced me to recognize. I sat staring at that little bump and decided it was time to cut it loose; time to move forward. Seconds later, that last, tiny little obstacle was untwisted and I could see what the yarn would finally become.

Having learned my lesson, I turned my attention to the remaining hanks. I was able to quickly finish the job of re-winding the yarn without creating another mess. I now have several balls of yarn ready to be formed into that lovely spring sweater. They serve as a reminder that with patience comes clarity; with clarity comes hope. Hope is actually the knot that ties everything together.

JANE

I believe that of all my father's accomplishments, it was his six children that made him the most proud. In my eulogy, I shared that my father built a family that does stand strong and does stand up for each other. On more than one occasion, I remember Dad telling me he was grateful that his children all got along with no significant family divisions; we enjoy each other. I'm pretty confident he would have found great joy in the family gathering together for my niece Megan's 30th birthday, just as we did my brother Bob's 60th a few weeks earlier. We shared time to celebrate these two milestones. Each event included close friends, but it was the gathering of family that made it clear how deeply we care for each other. Even though we all have a quirk or two that may annoy someone, we play well together. Without Dad, my siblings now keep me rooted to this earth, and I can't imagine my life without them. Which brings me to Jane.

My cousin, Jane, is the only child and daughter of my maternal Aunt Irene. The months following my mother's death, Barbie and I stayed with Aunt Irene and Uncle Merrick for the summer. I remember swimming at the golf club, the corner park, and countless games of "Cootie" with Jane. I can still see the sign above the ice cream store and it was Uncle Merrick who taught me how to play croquet. Barbie and I bunked with Jane and it was Aunt Irene who knelt beside us as we said bedtime prayers. Jane told me years later that for a few short months she felt she had sisters. With Labor Day came the return to our dad's care, but those weeks with Aunt Irene and Jane are remembered as being full of love.

In the following years, we did not see my mother's family frequently. Her sisters, fondly referred to as "The Aunts", were invited to all the big events: communions, graduations, weddings. Each time, these lovely women would break into tears when they spotted their little sister's four children. For my part, it was always a powerful reminder of a bond that was deeply ingrained in my psyche. Seeing Jane would immediately take me back to those walks to the ice cream store and croquet.

As adults, we saw each other even less frequently, mostly at funerals. Each time, Jane and I would promise to get together more often and I expressed my wish to visit Aunt Irene. Suffering with Alzheimer's, Irene has been in a long term care facility for a number of years and Merrick's health was failing. Caring for both her parents, alone, Jane was unable to attend my father's funeral. When her daughter called recently to tell me that Uncle Merrick had passed away, she let me know how distressed Jane was that she had missed paying her respects. When I went to pay mine, we spent two hours catching up and sharing our individual grief. We made a plan, actually picking a date to visit her mom. I knew Aunt Irene wouldn't know who I was, but she was in good health and I wanted to spend time with this woman who mothered me during one of the most critical times of my life. The day we picked was just a couple of weeks later on a Sunday. Sadly, Jane called on the Friday before to share her mother had passed away early that morning, of what can only be described as a broken heart. Jane believed that after Merrick's passing, Irene stopped caring to live.

In the span of 19 days, Jane lost both her parents. Unimaginable. Unimaginable to think that Jane has to cope with this devastating loss without the help of a brother or a sister. While Jane is supported by a loving husband and daughters, they didn't lose what she did. When Dad was dying, it was my five siblings that kept me sane; without them I would have dissolved into a puddle. During the wake, during the days following the funeral, it was this strong genetic bond that kept me standing upright. I know Jane has loving family and friends to guide her through this time, but as I walked back into the same funeral home I had visited just days before, I had one thought: How will she do it?

Amazingly enough, Jane was just fine. I was overwhelmed with her strength as she spoke of needing to manage the details of her parents' wishes and her ability to smile knowing they were once again together. She may not have the support of siblings, but Jane has an unfailing belief that the love of Irene and Merrick will continue to hold her up. We agreed, that with all our parents once more together, that there is one hell of party going on in heaven.

Last night's birthday party for Megan was a reminder that I'm blessed five times over. It was a living reminder of my father's legacy; the gift he gave to each of us. In post-party conversations this morning, the theme was the same: we need to celebrate often! We need to nurture this time together and not just because it is a holiday or someone's birthday. I was reminded that I waited too long to get in touch with Jane and I missed my opportunity to thank Aunt Irene one last time. Promises really don't matter unless we keep them. Relationships don't deepen unless we nurture them. And words left unsaid will never be heard.

SHUFFLE

Dad didn't believe in shuffling a deck of cards. When we played gin, I would shuffle for a few moments making sure that the previous hand was completely removed. Dad, on the other hand, shuffled the deck for just a few seconds. He felt that mathematically, shuffling made no difference; the next deal would be just as random. It made me crazy. During the last few months of his life, I did almost all the shuffling and there were times when Dad would just shake his head, wishing he could grab the cards from me. My win-loss ratio did not change.

I couldn't help thinking about Dad this past weekend when I desperately needed a change of scenery and headed to Carlisle; a long car ride alone to process the tangled emotions that have taken up residence in my heart. The grieving process for Dad has caused other loss issues to get stirred up, which I believed were long settled. My thoughts were all over the place. I had just visited with my maternal side, the Cassidys, and was thinking of how that connection remains fragile. I was thinking of family members who are struggling with stress and worry. I was thinking of Julie and her adjustment to leaving school and finding a new direction for her life. Heading to a town where I was happy, I pondered the years of my marriage before things got complicated. Mostly I struggled with an ever present sense of anxiety: I'm not moving forward in my life, I'm stuck.

You see, I was asked recently if I had forgiven Julie's father for his betrayal. My first response was to answer "Yes", because I'm certainly more than kind to him. Don't get me wrong, I often feel extremely angry at him, at his expectations of my friendship and support. That leads me to feeling angry at myself for not being clearer in my needs, in not setting clearer boundaries. I've permitted him access to my life that I don't want him to have. I feel guilty that my life is better since the divorce. The question becomes, am I not being honest with him, or am I not being honest with myself? I don't regret the divorce....EVER. I often struggle with finding the balance between compassion and enabling.

I had to reflect more on the question of forgiveness and what it truly means to forgive. Does it mean to forget, or does it mean to never feel the hurt, regret, or anger? Can we feel both anger and offer absolution? If so, does that mean that the relationship can continue in some way? When I ask to be forgiven, I acknowledge that I'm hoping the other person can accept my flaws and then move forward. What exactly does it mean when people say that forgiveness is what we do for ourselves, not for the other person? I thought of Dad asking for grace in the final days of his life. He told me he believed he had been a bad father and apologized. I continue to pray he found the peace he sought. I thought of Julie's father asking me to give him one more chance, and I remember my anger. Then I thought of my friend, Deirdre, believing that healing begins when we no longer see value in the pain. There it is. I need to stop finding a purpose in the misery. I'm the one who is responsible for keeping it in the present, when it needs to be in the past. I can only leave the hurt behind when I forgive.

At this point in my drive and internal emotional processing, Dad decided to again send me a message, to shuffle things up. The iPod was plugged into the radio, and I had a song list playing randomly. Not knowing what song was coming next, I was startled when suddenly Frank's voice filled the car: "Fly me to the moon, let me swing among the stars. Let me see what spring is like on Jupiter and Mars. In other words, please be true. In other words, I love you!" There was nothing random about that shuffle. It was one of Dad's favorite songs and he was (again) telling me to get on with the game, to be honest with myself and get moving. He was telling me that yes, the hand I was dealt has not always been fair, but when is it? He was also telling me that there is so much life beyond what I see.

As I exited the turnpike and paid the toll, I approached Carlisle with a sense of peace. I wasn't there to examine the past; all that has come before is simply what has come before. I was there to visit friends who are a loving source of joy in my life now. In that quiet moment, I could feel Dad smiling. He continues to guide me, to teach me about this life. He had shuffled ever so briefly, and we both had won.

POLISHING

One of my fondest childhood memories is of getting new Easter outfits. Christmas meant presents under the tree, but Easter meant new dresses, shoes, and gloves. All lined up in different pastel shades, sporting fancy hats, my sisters and I were quite the vision. When our patent leather shoes got scuffed, Dad taught us to rub them with Vaseline until we could again see our reflection. Man, that guy loved to polish shoes!

Dad had a shoe shine box with a hinged lid that held all his different polishes, rags, and brushes. Painted red, with colored letters that spelled "Shoe Shine" on the sides, it could be found at different times in the basement, his closet, or the garage workbench. I can still see Dad in the kitchen, buffing his shoes to a high gloss shine. Those black wingtips were ready to dance.

Sometime in the last 10 years, though I don't remember how, that small red chest came to be in my possession. It continues to hold all the necessary supplies to clean my footwear. The fading paint is almost completely worn off and the letters are barely visible. Recently, while polishing my black pumps, I got to thinking about where Dad may have gotten the tiny trunk. Clearly homemade, did Dad make it? Was the box possibly a high school wood working project? What was the story of that portable shoe shine stand?

Phoning Mom first, she knew only that Dad brought it to the marriage. Next, I called Dad's twin sister, Aunt Mary, who had no memory of the specific box but wondered if perhaps it had belonged to my grandfather. I then took a photo and emailed it to Dad's brother, hoping he could shed some light on its history. The image did not trigger any memory with Uncle Don, though he vaguely re-called having a similar one. Was it perhaps a joint project designed by the brothers as young boys?

With Dad's passing, I'd reached the end of the line. The only person who could tell me the story of the shoe shine box was Dad. Why had I never asked him about it? I vaguely remember jumping at the chance to own it, but had never inquired about its origin. I was saddened to realize how many stories I would never hear, how many answers I would never know.

I spent a lot of time with Dad in his last years but rarely did we talk about his life. We talked about mine, we talked about Julie, and we complained about the Browns. We argued politics, we discussed movies and music, and conversations about his health were constant. I'm ashamed to say that rarely did I think of asking Dad to tell me his stories. How much richer would my life be if I'd thought to ask him a few questions?

I wish I'd have asked what it was like to be a twin. Or which book was his all- time favorite. Who taught him to drive? What was the name of the first girl he kissed? What was Dad thinking when he walked each of his four daughters down the aisle? Did he really, as he told us on multiple car trips, paint the yellow line down the middle of almost every road we drove? But more importantly, what lessons did I fail to learn from him because I failed to ask for his wisdom? What could Dad have taught me about being a parent and being in love if I'd just asked?

I'm sure there were times I disappointed my father, but rarely did he let me know. When Dad was struggling with something I'd done, how did he manage those feelings? How did he keep from blocking the way when he saw me heading down a path that would cause pain? As a parent, how did Dad let go when he knew full well that I was going to fall?

Then I wondered how many times this man had his heart broken. I'm curious how he managed to open his heart to love a second time. When scared, how did he take the next step? In other words, when life was messy, how did Mike clean it up?

I want to imagine that he did it much like he polished shoes. He took his simple box filled with simple tools and simply got the job done. Dad probably didn't spend a lot of time wondering how to negotiate the maze of human emotions that confront us all, he just sat and quietly reflected on the task at hand.

If I could adjust that memory of seeing Dad buffing shoes in the kitchen, it would only be to insert myself into the picture. I'd put myself at the table on Sunday nights watching him arrange the tins of polish. Seeing him pick up a shoe, I would ask if he constructed and painted the iconic box. Instead, I will talk quietly with Dad while I get my own patent leathers ready for Easter. I'll get out the stained rags and the Vaseline and rub it into my fancy pumps. Closing my eyes, I'll imagine him teaching me his polishing tricks and telling me all the stories contained in that red shoe shine box. And I will listen.

SENSES

I remember the moment with all my senses. I can see my nieces, Megan and Bridget, playing in the kitchen. I can smell the chocolate cake my sister Barbara was baking. I can taste the tea I was drinking. I can hear the phone ringing and I can feel the receiver in my hand. I remember slipping to the floor, calling my father "Daddy", as I listened to the sound of his tears. It was the only time I ever heard my father cry, and it was the single moment when I felt the most loved. It was the moment he told me about Julie.

My husband and I were in Cleveland for his brother's wedding. After days of festivities, I was staying a bit longer to spend time with my family and again talked with my father about infertility. Another miscarriage had left me overwhelmed with sadness and frustration. We actually started the process for adoption by meeting with an attorney but had been told it was a long hard road. In those years, Dad had a small manufacturing business based in South Dakota and he was returning to Sioux Falls after his weekly visit home. He left with a heavy heart, feeling powerless to ease my pain.

Upon landing, Dad shared my plight with his secretary, Lynette, and learned of a young couple who had just given birth. Feeling they could not financially support this baby girl, the parents were looking to place the child for adoption. Dad, without my knowledge, went to them and suggested that I would be a great choice. In another moment of incredible love for a daughter, Julie's birth parents said "Yes." Twenty-four hours later, Dad was on the phone with me. As I sat on Barbie's kitchen floor, I was overwhelmed with love for my father, for a child I did not yet know, and for her parents. After begging a gate agent for a ticket, I arrived in South Dakota the next day and sat with Lori, Julie's birth mother. We both cried, knowing her sacrifice would mean pain for her and joy for me…complicated emotions that collided and resulted in my leaving the hospital with an infant daughter.

The connection Dad had with Julie was unique. Not many men get to meet their grand-daughter before her mother even knows she exists. I spent my first sleepless night as a parent in his home and turned his desk into a changing table. We celebrated Father's Day by watching golf and shopping for a car seat. There wasn't a card in the world that could express my feelings and I hope he knew the extent of my love for him. I have forever linked Julie's birthday with Father's Day and those early days spent in South Dakota.

As the years went by, Dad always referred to Julie as "the baby" and he loved telling the story of how she became a member of our family. When she and I returned to Sioux Falls in 2010 to meet her birth family, Dad couldn't wait to hear the details. Did he feel closer to Julie than to his other grandchildren? No. But Julie felt Grandpa's love in a special way, and she never failed to say "I love you."

Father's Day is approaching and this year falls on Julie's birthday. When talking about what we miss about Dad, Julie wondered what had happened to a bracelet he wore to combat his arthritis. I don't know if it actually helped with his pain but it was as much a part of his wardrobe as his endless supply of colorful golf shirts. A simple silver braid with a copper ball on each end, the bracelet graced Dad's wrist for more years than I can remember. I was surprised Julie had actually taken notice of it and tickled when she asked if Grandma might be willing to part with it. Touched that she wanted something belonging to Dad, I promised I would check it out with her grandmother.

As luck would have it, my timing was perfect. Mom was beginning to part with more of Dad's belongings and was pleased to pass the bracelet onto Julie. I imagine he would love the idea of Julie staying connected to him in this way. Plus, it will allow me to be reminded of him whenever I see it on her wrist. Never one to believe in coincidences, it seems like the perfect birthday present for Julie and the perfect way to honor his memory while holding on to my own.

Yet again, my senses come alive with memories of those early days in South Dakota. I can see Dad in his golf cap sitting in his living room holding Julie. I can smell the baby lotion and feel my dad touch my arm as he passes her to me. I can taste the salt of my happy tears. But mostly, it is through Julie, that I can forever hear my father say "I love you."

MATCH

Camping has never been high on my list of fun. I don't like sleeping on hard ground, peeing in holes, and I'm not very good at setting up a tent. On one of the only two camping trips I've endured, a friend taught me how to start a fire and shared the wisdom, "You can't light a fire with a wet match". As I enter the world of on-line dating, the truth of those words has never been more accurate.

Last year I spent a few months experimenting with this new age Cupid. I found the process to be filled with frustration, disappointment, and rejection. I let my initial subscription expire, deciding I didn't really know what I was seeking. After spending a number of months taking a long look at myself and relationship history, I again dipped my toe in the dating pool. First I signed up for a match-making site for people over 50. I didn't want to be competing with women 20 years my junior but wasn't at all prepared for flirts from men of my father's age. I again let my days run out before switching to the site that claims to be responsible for the most marriages. The name of the site is appropriate because a match is a spark used to ignite a longer burning flame. The problem is, after only six weeks, I'm completely burned out.

Here are the rules. You shop. You post a picture and write a profile communicating your exercise habits, interests, and shoe size. If you're smart, you indicate your love of all music, sports, and the willingness to do anything new. Most profiles refer to perfect bodies, perfect kids, and perfect dogs. Finally, don't forget to highlight your romantic side and love of the outdoors. It seems as if the woods are full of single people just waiting to meet!

Based on all that information, members can send a wink, flirt, or a message. If you're the sender, you wait. Will the object of your interest respond in kind or just ignore the gesture? Worse yet, will you get "blocked", meaning you can't even look at their profile again? You can be rejected even before the person knows your bad habits. Even if you have worn your best dress.

As the recipient, you have the same options. If the person doesn't fit your height requirements, religious beliefs, share your hobbies, or has a moustache...a simple tap on the delete button removes them from your life; you move on to the next one. It's window shopping for love.

The problem is, we're much more complicated creatures than we can ever communicate digitally, and there is a huge advantage of first meeting in person. The memory of catching someone's eye across a crowded room and holding the look just long to keep it interesting, is just that, a memory. When relationships start by being in the same place, there's the experience of being drawn in by who the person is, not by whom you want them to be. If there's a connection, you begin to look deeper, to want to know more. After getting to know each other, the decision is made if the imperfections can be accepted and accommodations made. Maybe they can and maybe they can't. Hopefully, there's the effort at supporting and caring, at overlooking the flaws. Once in love, when hair turns grey, when a few pounds are added, you still see the soul of the person. But when you are starting over at 50+, there seems to be no time to allow this natural process to occur. Instead, people rush to judgment, rush to love, and rush to move on.

I recently met a fine man and after three very pleasant evenings, we each began to have our doubts. We discussed how I live too much in my heart and perhaps he lives a bit too much in his head. His practicality was in direct opposition to my romanticism. As we talked, this man felt that he'd been blind to the idea that I could already have an emotional investment. It seems I was blind to the value of time. He ultimately apologized for being focused on the process rather than the end goal. The reality is, the apology belongs on my side of the table. He was doing it right, simply focusing on sharing time. My heightened expectations created an uncomfortable situation and the loss is clearly mine. What I'm looking for is to work in tandem with someone to create a full life; to move together at the same pace and discover the best of ourselves.

So here I sit, rejecting and being rejected. I want to believe my profile and pictures accurately capture my intelligence, spirit, and passion. I trust those extra pounds that appeared when Dad died (grief and chocolate are a natural couple) will be accepted as I continue to get rid of them. I hope that someone is willing to look past the surface to see my soul, and I want to believe that I'll do the same.

I don't want to light a match. I want to do it the old fashioned way; by rubbing two sticks together to create the warmth we all crave. I want to nurture the flame so that when the rains come, when the wind blows, it doesn't again go out.

LEAVES

For years, my family lived in a home that overlooked the Cleveland Metroparks, known as "the valley." The property was landscaped with huge maple and oak trees and what seemed like acres of pachysandra. The months of October and November meant days of endless raking and many a Saturday morning started with Dad handing us the dreaded tool. I remember taking it from his hands with a polite scowl, as my weekend was ruined before it even started. My siblings and I worked to create piles of leaves that were transferred onto tarps, dragged to the edge of the valley, and dumped over the side. While I grew to hate raking, I grew to love the sound of leaves crunching under my feet and the stunning hues of the season. During a recent drive through the valley, I recalled those mornings of raking when I noticed the trees were beginning to change their colors. I thought that for many, autumn represents the end of a season. For me, this year, it's a new beginning.

I'm moving. In a few short weeks, Julie and I will leave this little house behind and settle into our new home. This dwelling has been a great place for both of us to heal from the wounds inflicted by divorce and it's time to spread our wings. We move to a place where my best friend, Deirdre, grew up, a home that held nothing but love for over 50 years. The other day I walked through the empty rooms of the house alone, and I could feel the essence of the life shared; the peace coming through the walls. Knowing this home held no animosity, no anger, I felt a sense of hope and an incredible calmness. I strolled over to the large picture window in the family room and flung back the drapes to let in the sun. Looking out onto the back yard, I noticed the bed of pachysandra at the base of a large tree. Flashing back, I felt a bit of dread at the thought of raking leaves out of that tricky ground cover. Then I smiled at those memories of long afternoons clearing debris, knowing that in a way, those hours of raking prepared me for this change.

I have spent more than half my life living on the same two mile stretch of road. From my childhood home, to my own apartment, to the marital dwelling, and finally to the house Julie and I landed in after the divorce, I've navigated the many seasons of this life. I can remember the smells of my elementary school, the trick or treat route, and where to find the best Christmas trees. I know exactly

121

how to time the lights along the main drag and have known the same mailman for many years. I run into old neighbors at the grocery store and I once found my dog returning to the house we lived in while still married. The view from the car is stunningly familiar and, in some ways, has kept me from seeing new options. Packing up the boxes of my life, I ponder all I'm leaving behind.

I leave this house to create a new home, to again feel connected to my space. I wash my hands of the anger, disappointment, and lack of trust that followed me here. I'm letting go of the self-doubt and I leave behind the memories of betrayal. I'm dumping the fear of taking a risk with my heart. There is no room in my packed boxes for any of it. It all gets raked onto that tarp and dumped over the edge. I'm taking only those things that nurture my soul and connect me to my hopes.

I can't wait to find a new place to get take-out Chinese. I'll need a new library card and have miles of new bike trails to explore. I need to pick a new favorite watering hole and I welcome getting lost on the back roads on the way to the grocer. Until I find my way in the dark, I'll run into a few walls on my way to the bathroom, and will greet each day surrounded by the spirit of love that resides in the eaves. My morning tea will find me watching the squirrels in the front yard and I'll take Christmas cookies to new neighbors. In the spring, I can see what flowers pop up and plant perennials that will bloom each year. The ride to work will be longer, but I'll have more time for my morning chat with Dad.

Despite the tedious work that is the moving process, I embrace this new journey. Never have I been more ready to leave my comfortable path and explore new routes. There are no ghosts going with me. Dad's photo will be the last item taken down from the shelf and he will ride shot-gun to my new place. This time, I think I will hand him the rake!

HELEN

Back in my Carlisle days, before there was Julie, there was Helen. Helen was a cool old broad whom I met in a 6:00 a.m. water aerobics class. Helen could jog through that water faster than I and she had a good 40 years on me. We became fast friends, often going to lunch together and floating in her backyard swimming pool. She and her husband, Bill, had a nice little 10 acre spread and for several years they gave my husband and me a large garden plot in which to grow vegetables. We planted corn, potatoes, squash, tomatoes, beans, all of which we canned. Then there was the year of the onions.

My husband was convinced that real gardeners grew onions from seeds. As the supportive wife, I dutifully helped dig tiny holes and dropped in the packaged seeds. Helen sat on her porch, drinking coffee, laughing her ass off. When pressed, she promptly told me that onions were never going to grow from those seeds. Not to be deterred, my "farmer", daily made the trip to water our crops and check for the onion sprouts. Each day he came home discouraged and each morning when I saw Helen, she just shook her head. When she learned my husband was out of town, she showed up in her Cadillac convertible to haul me off to the hardware store where we purchased several bags of onion sets (small onions with sprouts that "real farmers" use to grow onions). We spent the afternoon planting the sets where the onion seeds lay dormant. When my husband showed up a few days later to check on his vegetables, the joy on his face was as wide as the garden plot. He believed those sprouts had come from those seeds and was over the moon. We never told him the truth, and I never really thanked Helen for her wise friendship.

That friendship continued through the birth of Julie and the sudden death of Bill. Helen was never quite the same after Bill died. In over 50 years together, they had never spent a night separate from each other. Helen had, rarely, in her life, left the boundaries of Carlisle. She had great difficulty navigating her way through life at that point, and I noticed more and more confusion on her part. When we moved away from Carlisle, my communication with Helen gradually dwindled until we lost touch. On return trips I learned she no longer lived on that same 10 acres and no one seemed to know where she had gone. I assumed she had died but no one was able to confirm it for me. On my last visit, I decided that there was only one place Helen would be if she had passed away...next to Bill. So, on my way out of town, I stopped at the cemetery and finally found Helen. She died eight years ago, just days before Thanksgiving. I wept at her grave. I cried out of sadness for the years lost and out of anger at myself for never letting Helen know how much her friendship meant to me.

I know it's traditional on Thanksgiving Day to count blessings and look to the heavens in gratitude, and I daily recognize my blessings. Today I want to give thanks in a slightly different way; by thanking you, my friends, for what you have brought to my life. I want to thank you for the times you helped me get out of bed when I thought I never would. Thank you for the weekends you moved me from one house to another and most recently to another. The walls you have painted, the showers you have fixed, the toilets you have replaced, have all eased my burden. I'm blessed with the gift of your time to take long walks, the times you held my hand and wrapped me up in warm hugs. You taught me that a good book is to be cherished and a bad one does not have to be finished. Thank you for long Scrabble games, the Polar Bear Plunge, and the Jell-O Museum. You pushed me beyond my own mental limitations by making me get back on my bike with 20 miles to go. Thank you for being at the finish line. Because of you, I know that walls can be climbed and jumping over fire doesn't burn. I know that Shangri-La is as close as the back yard. For the countless hours of conversation about life and love and tolerating my never-ending questions, I'm forever grateful. Thank you for trivia nights, movies, Toby Keith, concerts and dancing. You are the music of my life.

We have cried out of sadness and laughed until we peed our pants. Whether it's been mimosas on the beach, wine on the front porch, or margaritas after work, we drowned our sorrows and tipped a glass to our successes. You have instinctively known when to show up on my front doorstep. Words cannot express the feelings for those moments you offered to spend the night and the times you actually did. Thank you for teaching me that family is far more than genetics. I'm in awe of your many talents and your willingness to share them. I'm honored you find me worthy of hearing your life stories and continue to allow me to be a part of new chapters. You've been my scarecrow, tin-man, lion, and wizard, always helping me find my way home. The ice cream, chocolate, and cups of hot tea are reminders of how sweet this life is, and you never let me forget that love is always possible. Because of you, I will forever believe in angels.

I don't shed tears when I slice onions. I think of Helen. I think of how we were unlikely friends who shared some unlikely moments. I can still see her sitting on the porch laughing, and I remember giggling like little girls as we planted those onion sets. As I spend the day with those I love, I will remember Helen. I will remember her humor and wisdom and the years of keeping our onion secret. I will finally thank her for planting a seed that has continued to sprout a bounty of blessings.

STEPS

Every day for the past year I've longed to talk to Dad, to share the daily details I use to share on Sundays. Since I can't, I think I will send up this letter:

Dear Dad,

I remember how often you told me I began walking when I was just 8 months old. I imagine you down on your knees with open arms to catch me. No doubt those first early steps were shaky and I'm equally sure that as often as I walked, I fell down. That seems to be the perfect analogy for the journey of the last year. Yes, it has been a year since I last held your hand, kissed your cheek and heard your voice. Three hundred and sixty-five days since I took the first steps to living a life without you. It feels like yesterday. I want to fill you in on the happenings of the last year and I apologize if I'm telling you things you already know. I wonder about that a lot: do you actually see everything that is going on here or are you too busy with whatever it is that happens in the afterlife?

I still miss you every day. I tend to feel your absence the most when I'm alone in the car. Something about driving makes me think of you. Sometimes it's a song or passing the family home on Macbeth Drive. It happens when I'm alone with my own thoughts or because a vivid memory bursts into my awareness. Now that clementine oranges are back in season, I think of you eating them as fast as I could peel them. Of course, there is South Dakota when Julie was born, and one private conversation that week is tattooed on my soul.

I'm no different than a million other people who would like one more minute with someone they love. I have no idea what I'd do with those sixty seconds, so I've cherished the time you let me know that you're still with me. I remember the day I was driving to the cemetery in Huron and you again played Sinatra on my iPod, the very second I passed your hometown of Vermilion. I recall the morning I saw your hand in the car when I was driving to work. I could actually see you reach for something right in front of the steering wheel. These moments have brought both tears to my eyes and a smile to my heart. Whether you can hear me or not, I love talking to you and imagining your responses. I missed our inevitable banter during the election and I knew exactly what words you would have used on that Tuesday evening in November.

This first round of holidays was tough. On Christmas Eve we brought back the tuxedos and party dresses, and Bob was a great patriarchal host. Your spirit was everywhere and I hope you saw the balloon of wishes we launched on a perfectly clear night. My wish remains the same: to feel your presence in my life every day. I did the Polar Bear Plunge on New Year's Eve, and it was a cold way to wash away the pain of the year and start fresh. We've all celebrated growing another year older without your homemade birthday cards, which you spent hours making personal for each of us. On your birthday, your children gathered to raise a glass in your memory. For some reason, believe it or not, I didn't see Father's Day coming and it nearly did me in. But I have found great comfort in spending time with the family as I see so much of you in each of your kids and grandkids.

Even though I no longer play gin, I'm betting you have run into a few of your card playing buddies and are enjoying some real competition again. I smile knowing you can hold your cards without dropping any and that your coin jar is once again getting full. I also miss the Sunday afternoons we watched the Browns lose. I'm sure you're not at all surprised to learn that they are again in last place. Amazingly, they actually beat the Steelers last Sunday!

But this year has also been about moving forward; about honoring your life by living mine. I actually moved away from that two mile stretch of Wooster Road where I spent more than half my life. I'm in a home with no emotional ghosts and plenty of room to build more happy memories. I sleep well here, Dad. I feel safe, warm, and happy. Your photograph graces the piano you gave Julie, and your bracelet graces her wrist. Julie's journey in this world seems complicated, but she is finding her way; I'm grateful that you and my other guardian angels continue to light her path. She misses you, Dad, and I hope you know how special you are to her.

In case you haven't heard, I was published! The story I wrote about taking Julie to meet her birth family was accepted by an adoption journal. It was amazing to see my name listed as a contributing author on the inside cover! Would you have ever guessed that my ramblings would turn me into an author? I do have one regret: I wish I had submitted the piece as Susan

Emmerich, the name you gave me. You see, the thought of changing my name creeps often into my brain since you died. Part of me feels it's the final step I have to take to complete the healing process from both the divorce and your death. I know. I know. I can just hear you telling me to get over myself and get on with things, but the name Emmerich holds no pain for me. It's a good STRONG name and I want to again feel that my name really represents who I am. Being an Emmerich in name again will keep me connected to you. Silly? Maybe. But I always was your emotional child, thinking more with my heart than my head.

Speaking of my heart, I started dating and you would enjoy some of the stories that came out of the online match game. There were plenty of missteps and lots of dashed expectations, but there seems to be a special one, Dad. I like him. You would, too. He's a good man…kind. I regret the two of you will never meet. Sorry, but like me, he's a liberal. Yet I think even you would approve, because he does golf! Being with him is a reminder that I deserve to be treated well. I don't yet know where this relationship is headed, but today it feels right. I've learned that I don't have to settle for anything less than everything. Having that insight is more than a tiny step for me, and I'm no longer afraid.

About golf, how does it feel to once again swing a club and walk the greens? Many times over the last year I've smiled, knowing you are no longer in pain; no longer limited by your own body. My heart leaps with joy when I think of you throwing back a beer at the 19th hole after shooting under 80.

Somehow, Dad, despite losing you, this past year I have found myself. I wrote, I moved, I risked my heart. I even got rid of my wedding rings. I'm letting go of all those things that keep me stuck, keep me from standing on my own two feet. I stumble sometimes and take brief trips into self-pity, but then I remember how many times you got up from your wheelchair, determined to walk and simply took one step.

Today I plan to listen to your music: Sinatra, Stewart, and Streisand. I plan to drink a glass of good merlot, tipping it to the heavens. I hope the tears I shed today are brief and that when I lay my head down tonight you see that I'm okay. I'll think of all that has happened in the past year and about the year to come. I have a visit to Mount Rushmore and walking a half marathon in my sights. Beyond that, I plan to wait and see what this next year has in store for me and walk the path I'm given.

Last year, Laura gave me a small decorative plate that simply says: "Take the First Step." It sits on my dresser as a reminder to take each day as it's offered and continue the journey. I often think of you when I see that plate because I imagine you saying those same words when I was that 8 month old clinging to the coffee table: "Susie let go. Just take the first step. I gotcha." I'm not running yet, Daddy, but I am moving forward. I know you will forever be waiting to catch me when I fall.

STARS

Growing up, decorating the Christmas tree was a tedious affair. After waiting for what seemed like hours for Dad to not only untangle the strings of lights, but then to test each colored bulb until they lit up, my siblings and I would finally get to hang our favorite ornaments. When it came time for the tinsel, Dad insisted that it be hung by individual strands. It was torture. Being kids, we were content with throwing clumps of the stuff onto the branches and often cheated by hanging two or three strands together. Dad, however, was going for the magical sparkling effect that comes with patience. Only then could the angel be placed gently at the top of the tree, creating the vision of her looking down on a thousand sparkling stars. With the room lights turned off, it was indeed a glorious sight. That memory, and the events of the past year, has me thinking a lot about stars. What exactly are those flickering gems to which we launch our wishes?

Science has taught me that stars are massive balls of plasma (very hot gas, for those of you who may have forgotten), held together by gravity. I remember learning the closest star to us is the sun, providing most of the energy for the earth. Points of light in the night sky, stars have guided explorers and travelers for eons. Visible as only tiny dots that seem close enough to touch, I'm always amazed that we can so clearly see something that is, literally, light years away. Overwhelmed by the sheer vastness of the sky, I find few things beat a night walk under a blanket of light shared with someone I love.

Some fork lore suggests our loved ones can be found in the skies. To gaze at the heavens is to gaze into the souls of our ancestors and to know they are watching over us. The light that burns is their love and protection and, when they twinkle, I've often imagined they are laughing both at and with us as we journey through this earthly life. Each year at this time I search the vast darkness for Dad and claim the most luminous for him. Knowing that he is among those points of heaven make the holidays just a teeny bit easier because I know the tinsel on Heaven's Christmas tree is exquisitely hung.

This past year, Dad has been joined by four more souls that are dear to the hearts of people whom I love. Irene, Merrick, Josephine, and Ann Marie have all joined that canvas of lights for this holiday season. I've wept for my cousin and friends, knowing full well the depth of their pain at a time we all celebrate the love of family. Their Christmas trees are just a little less bright as they mourn the passing of their parents. For two of them, this loss came within a few days/weeks of the holidays, and they face them with still healing wounds. I imagine that their faith is just a wee bit shaky as they struggle to find joy in a time of great sorrow.

Yet it is my faith that's taught me a single star can represent a thousand years of hope; that a single star guided three wise men to Bethlehem to protect the newborn king. What a glorious reminder that the love we feel in this life is a gift that we can't always see; that we can't always explain with science or stories. It just is. Love has no ending, even when we can no longer touch those we cherish the most. It is faith that's taught me that the love of those I miss burns on and can always be felt through the care I give to others.

Oddly enough, I don't have a Christmas tree this year. Having just settled from the move, the idea of getting and decorating a tree seemed daunting. So with the help of dear friends (and more than a little wine), my house is ablaze with lights. My bathroom looks like a winter wonderland of white lights and snowflakes. Doors and windows are framed with strings of colored stars that are attached with push pins and duct tape and serve as branches on which Julie and I hung our favorite ornaments. Lights are draped across my mantle, adorned with Santas, and they provide just enough glow to illuminate the Nativity. I love looking at each of these reminders that new traditions can be built on the history of my life.

My favorite holiday decoration was a simple idea by Madeline. She took a handful of gold stars resembling wands and placed them in a simple clear glass vase. They sit alone on my kitchen table and I can't help but think of the souls now decorating the halls of Heaven. Each glittery star serves to remind me that I'm loved in more ways than I can count. I'm surrounded by those who have gone before me and blessed by all those in my life now.

When I look to the heavens on Christmas Eve, I'll remember that stars continue to burn for thousands of years without ever going out. Finding the bright spot that is Dad, I will thank him for illuminating my path. Instead of throwing clumps of wishes his way, I will gently hang each, one at a time, on the points of his star.

RONNIE

Ronnie Beeler kissed me in the back seat of his mother's car. We were seven years old and I knew he was going to plant one on me because my eyes were wide open. I also knew I was in love with him. Ronnie moved away within a few months of that intimate moment, and I never saw him again. I was heartbroken and didn't kiss another boy for nine years. That time his name was George, and we were standing on my back stoop. When he leaned in, my eyes were closed and afterwards, I never wanted to kiss a guy again. Feeling nothing, I thought it was gross and couldn't wait to get inside the house. I didn't go out with George again. I was definitely not in love.

I wonder, is love a choice? Is it possible to turn this most mysterious of feelings off and on? Can we pick and choose for whom we fall, and can we decide not to love? Where does it go if not nurtured, or when it's not returned?

It wasn't love at first sight with my husband. Second maybe, but not first. The whirlwind that was our romance resulted in being married exactly one year from the day we met. Walking up that aisle, I felt no doubt, no hesitation. I was head over heels and beaming. Only much later did I begin to question if I'd missed some warning signs of future challenges during the year leading up to our nuptials. I don't think so and I don't ever regret getting married. I made a choice based on what I knew and felt at that point.

I held on to that loving feeling for many years as I tried to save the marriage and was surprised, years after the divorce, to wake up one morning and realize that the love was gone. What happened? Did I choose to not feel the emotion any longer, or had it simply faded from my heart? Had the feeling been driven away; how had passion become indifference?

I loved Julie from the first moment Dad told me she existed. I loved her on the plane ride to South Dakota and when I saw her through the nursery window. I didn't need nine months to bond, as I would have given my life for hers the second I held her. I clearly remember laying Jules down that first night and whispering those precious words into her ear. Did I choose that feeling? It has never faded, never been questioned. I didn't give birth to my daughter, but I feel bound to her in a way I feel with no one else.

Is romantic love vastly different than familial love? Or am I confused by passion? What is the sense of commitment I feel for my friends, because I do choose them…carefully. On the other hand, I didn't choose my family, yet they are part of my life blood and, at times, I feel my very breath is dependent on them.

How is it we decide to whom we give pieces of our heart? The romantic in me wants to believe this powerful emotion sneaks up on us and is always a gift. My spiritual side believes that love is God within each of us. It's natural, easy, and without risk. I don't know if it's been a choice and I lean toward feeling that love has no rules and requires no work. But the cynic in me worries; love is risky and can fade as quickly as it comes. I, like so many, have been hurt by the very emotion that has blessed my life, and I'm guilty of wondering if it's really worth it.

There seems to be no answer to the question of whether or not love is a choice. I can argue both sides and I can raise countless questions in search of an answer. What I do believe to my core, is that people come into our lives for a reason. How long they stay is the choice, as is what we do with that time. I know I feel and give love more freely than perhaps I should, wearing my heart on my sleeve. I have no intention of changing, and I accept the implied risk.

I never told Ronnie Beeler that I loved him. I'm not even sure I understood what that meant when I was seven. But I remember Ronnie, and I remember that kiss. So is love a choice? I don't know. For me, maybe it's as simple as whether or not I keep my eyes open.

WALKING

Years ago, while living in Philadelphia, an eye doctor had an interesting theory on why I was nearsighted. According to him, the problem was directly related to walking early. Since I took my first steps at just 8 months, I failed, in his opinion, to develop the appropriate level of depth perception. This led to a lifetime of nearsightedness and is probably why I can't hit a golf ball. Yet once I began walking, I moved fast. In many ways I've never slowed down.

I love to walk. Being outside, exploring new neighborhoods and sharing time with the dog, I walk with purpose and a clear expectation of where I'm headed. I want to log a certain distance at a certain pace and when alone, I love the solitude of my own thoughts. Some friends don't like walking with me; they complain my steps are too long and my pace too fast. Slowing down makes me feel I'm not getting anywhere, and if I move at my speed, I sense I'm making my partner uncomfortable. As it turns out, I tend to do the same thing in relationships, which is causing me to pause and look around. Damn.

Lately, I'm feeling out of sorts, uncomfortable in my own skin. I have a dozen theories as to why this is but nothing I can completely wrap my brain around. Some days I think it is post-divorce. Others I think it is post-Dad. There has been a slight shift in how I approach my life, a subtle change in my expectations of myself and others. I think it's in large part due to not living my own life, but trying to live the life I want. I'm walking too fast and not paying attention to where I am, too focused on where I want to be. In the process, I find myself walking alone.

It took me a long time to get comfortable being on my own, to recognize the value of time spent with just me. As I adjusted to life as a single person, I found a balance between social and solitary evenings. I took pleasure in discovering my adventurous side, while also learning to relish the weekends when I had no plans. Content in crocheting for days and not leaving the house, a blanket, the couch, and a frozen pizza were all I needed. These solo days didn't happen all the time and were buried treasure. Yet for the last few months, I dread those same weekends and evenings, finding myself staring at unread books and balls of yarn. I'm unsure of how to occupy my heart and mind when I don't have plans. Alone with my own thoughts can be a dangerous place as I stray from the present moment to the unknown.

Therein lies the problem: I'm scared to death of finding myself, 90-years old, with no one to hold my hand when I'm stooped over and eating applesauce. I'm terrified I'll be the woman whom no one misses for days. I'm more than worried that I'll never again know the feeling of being loved, of being cherished. Maybe I'm moving fast in the hopes I won't notice the fears following me.

The result is constantly looking behind to see if the people I want to share this life with are still with me. When they slow down to look at the landscape, I feel a sense of worry and loss. I actually feel left behind, fearing I will be alone. I traveled that road of self-doubt and loss for a very long time, and I'm not going back. How do I once again find the life balance that guided me for so long? Could it be as simple as just slowing down?

I recently agreed to walk a half marathon in May. When I downloaded the training schedule, it recommended slower easier walks during the week, building up to longer more intense work-outs on weekends. The guidelines actually used the word "stroll." I wonder if that isn't exactly how I need to approach this life phase and any new relationship. To make it to the finish line, I need to share the journey with others who are moving at the same pace. Getting there first means nothing if I can't share the experience.

Was that eye doctor right? I don't have a clue. I think he was actually a whack job. My vision issues have nothing to do with early walking and everything to do with watching where I'm going. I need to make sure that I look just far enough ahead to not fall down.

LUGGAGE

For as long as I can remember, I have over packed. Whether it's a day at the beach or a week in New York, I take too much stuff. I hate the idea of having to decide days in advance what I plan to wear. I worry about all the different weather possibilities and want to make sure I have everything I could ever need. For a beach vacation, most folks pack a bathing suit, shorts, and several t-shirts. I pack two suits, four pairs of shorts, jeans, sweaters, t-shirts, and a dress. Add in several different styles of footwear and you can see why my luggage usually needs to be checked curbside. If the bag is too heavy, you have to pay even more than the standard fee, and the toll is a hefty one. It's the same in matters of the heart.

I spent the last four months with a man who is incredibly kind, gentle, and interesting. To me, there seemed no end to the possibilities and I felt glorious. Each time I saw him, my heart would sing and I was willing to offer it up on a silver platter. I held nothing back. I was finally in a place where I was willing to take a risk, and I allowed myself to feel hopeful. I gave myself permission to trust, to dream, to believe. Hell, I fell in love. I may once again have over packed.

A very wise friend kept cautioning me to take along some logic to balance out the intense emotion. Knowing me well he, better than anyone, could see that I was at risk of being hurt if I wasn't paying attention to the lessons I so painfully learned in my 25 year marriage. He kept encouraging me to make sure I wasn't compromising my needs simply because it felt good. I was regularly forced to examine whether I was communicating what I needed and not falling into the old pattern of being more concerned with the needs of others.

Each time I felt that pull, I was able to manage the feeling, manage what I call my emotional "tics", or landmines. That was until this past weekend when I learned this man and I are not sharing the same journey. We might be looking to reach the same destination but are on different paths. The trip may be reaching a sudden, unexpected conclusion. The prick to my heart is huge and all the insecurities contained in that luggage have been unpacked and strewn everywhere.

As I look them over, my first and immediate reaction is to

think I'm lacking: I'm not cute enough, skinny enough, not lovable…all the things I was told in my marriage and believed deeply for so long. My second thought is that maybe my relationship anxieties haven't been as managed as I hoped and I presented as too needy. Since I hadn't really asked for much, how could that be? Lastly, I wonder if I'm just not deserving of the kind of relationship I crave. All deeply ridiculous thoughts. My head recognizes the flaw in reasoning but my heart just feels pain. My satchel is heavy as I ponder this never ending conflict: finding the balance between emotions and needs.

So what is it? Why does what I want keep slipping through my hands? There's no answer that will provide the comfort I seek. But I know this: there's no blame to be laid anywhere. It's not my baggage that caused the problem. If anything my past is telling me to trust my soul, trust that my needs are important. There are things in that bag that are necessary and valuable to protecting my heart, like my passion and resiliency. The challenge is in using those resources to guard my heart while fighting the urge to lock it up once more.

Yes, it's been a glorious four months. I had a great time. I put it all on the table and it felt good, it felt right. Actually, it still does which is why my head and heart will, for the immediate future, remain in conflict. In all honesty, I wouldn't do anything differently. I'll continue to pack everything I may need and bring everything along. Is there a fee for that? Yep, and I'm not quite sure what this is going to cost me. But after a reasonable layover, I plan to pick up my bag and keep moving.

BUTTONS

That memory of my mother's coat with the large gray buttons is buried deep in my psyche. I was sitting on the floor in my grandparents' home and she leaned over to kiss me goodbye. Already sick with cancer, she was headed to a doctor's appointment. Words that every parent recites when leaving are forever burned in the recesses of my brain: "I love you, I'll be back soon." If I saw her again, I don't recall; I do recall those buttons. They are a powerful reminder of an overwhelming loss and I often think of them when I'm sorting through my jar of colorful fasteners. Stored in my spare room closet is a blue mason jar full of different buttons, a collection of cast offs in all different colors and sizes. Periodically I need to dig through them to find just the right replacement for that cuff or waistband. This week a different kind of button, an emotional one, got pushed. Hard.

Recent events have left me feeling a bit off kilter and everything is ticking me off. Little things that wouldn't annoy me are looming large. No matter the issue, my first reaction is to be pissed. Who gets mad when the bananas are too brown? All my emotional triggers now seem to be on a motion detector and it doesn't take much to set one off. So when my former husband made a selfish decision, I felt the buttons pop. It doesn't really matter what the decision was, it just matters that he again chose his comfort over Julie's. Suddenly, I was right back in the mess of our troubled past.

I was surprised and scared by the depth of my anger and finally slammed shut the door on any remaining feelings of compassion. Horrible images filled my head for several hours as I pondered what I would do if he showed up at my door. Yet I was also briefly overwhelmed with sadness for the loss of a soul I once loved. Saddened with being reminded that perhaps my devotion had been misplaced for so many years, I found myself weeping in the office of a colleague. The tears were necessary before I could once again feel the anger was justified. Just to be clear, I don't like being angry.

Julie's father has been absent from my life for several months. I previously worked to maintain a cordial relationship with him but found that to do so meant losing part of myself. Old patterns are hard to break and each communication found me returning to my co-dependent ways. The decision not to have any contact was difficult and sad, but correct. I worried about the impact on Julie, yet knew she was old enough to have her own relationship with her dad. Cutting the cord, I began to feel stronger, better, lighter.

Julie relies on my strength to guide us both through life's challenging moments. Over the last 30 years, I've been told more than once by co-workers that my confidence is intimidating and students believe I'm wise and intelligent. Yet, deep in my heart is this mass of insecurity and doubt that rears its ugly head at the most inopportune moments. However briefly, I allow myself to listen to those doubts before I temporarily kick them to the curb. Never one to leave them there, I pick up those negative thoughts and tuck them securely back into my subconscious.

It follows that I'm the only one who can move them aside. I'm blessed by so many people who appreciate my gifts and are willing to share theirs with me. My family has never once let me down and are the pillars of my soul. I'm constantly boosted by the faith that others have in me and the stories with which I have been entrusted. Those are the buttons that I need to push. Those are the triggers that should be on a sensor and the ones to determine my direction in this world. Mostly, those are the memories that I should cling to in my mind. My mother didn't leave me on that day; she left trying to get well.

These days, when I need to mend a shirt, I often take that jar and dump it out on top of the guest room bed. When spread out on the quilt, they are a wonderful collection of memories and stories, some of which I'm sure I've forgotten. Each is unique in its ability to trigger a thought, an emotion. They are witness to the fact that this life is held together by the threads of mistakes, regrets, hopes, and joys. I'm going to need a bigger jar.

ROPES

Back in the days of blue one-piece uniforms and daily gym classes, there was one time of year I dreaded: the annual rope climb. You remember, having to grab ahold of a thick bristly rope that dangled from the ceiling, you had to pull yourself up as far as possible. The goal was to use your upper body to pull your full weight as you simultaneously locked your ankles around the rope. Every year I felt a sense of panic as I watched my friends easily navigate what was an impossible task for me. I never got off the ground. No matter how hard I worked, I was never able to reach the top, never able to get more than a foot off the floor. I always imagined that the view from the top was incredible and could not be experienced from the ground. My hands grew raw from trying to pass the test and every year I was defeated. The following year, the rope again beckoned, and I again believed I could do it.

Over the last six weeks, my hands are sore from holding on to something that was not mine. The man I thought had ended our relationship didn't quite do so until last night and, in the interim, I chose to hope. Ignoring some significant warning signs that, in retrospect, were screaming at me, I refused to let go and my arms are exhausted. I am wondering why I'm so blind to what is right in front of me. Why do I hang on long after it is obvious that I should let go?

The answer is simple: I'm addicted to hope. I hang on because to my core, I believe that what I want to happen, will. The universe will eventually align itself in my favor if I just wait patiently. Incredibly unproductive thinking; the result of living for years in the shadow of someone else's needs. It's a difficult pattern to break, and keeps me from making the changes necessary to actually embrace a healthy relationship. If I don't stop hoping for what I want to happen, I can't possibly be ready for what may await me.

In this case, I refuse to carry the burden alone. As kind and generous as this man is, he dangled the rope, allowing me to believe we could move forward; that we were moving forward but at a slower pace. His words didn't match his actions and I was foolish to trust what he said rather than what I was feeling. What I felt was way too much anxiety. When we were together, he made me feel like the most important person in the world, but each time he walked out the door I never quite believed he'd be back. I should have paid attention. I should have let go of the rope on my own instead of waiting for it to be pulled away. Rarely have I felt this kind of anxiety in my life. It was a new feeling and I struggled with how to manage. Ignoring my instincts, I failed to pay attention to not getting what I need, not feeling safe in asking for it. Instead I just hung on, hoping.

The anxiety is gone. I don't wonder if he's coming back...he isn't. The feeling is one of sadness. Now, THAT I know how to deal with. Sadness and loss are like old friends that periodically need to pay me a visit.I know how to manage these familiar emotions and I know that eventually they will fade to the background. Pushed out by my blessings and my ability to move forward, they will be replaced by my strength and desire to do something new, something that will make me feel beautiful. I don't know what that is yet, but I'm sure the universe will place it in front of me. I just have to keep my eyes open.

I always imagined that the view from the top of the rope was incredible. I figured once I made it, I would be able to see things that people down below were missing. I never did climb that rope in high school. But here's the thing: I still passed gym class with an "A." Maybe the take away from the last few months is that I don't want to climb the rope alone. If I grab on, I want someone with me as a backup. If I don't have a spotter to catch me then I need to let go before I get too high; before I leave the gym floor. If I choose to stay on the ground, the view is just as stunning.

PARIS

When my principal wanted a favor I expected him to ask me to do one of my least favorite tasks, provide data. Bracing for the request to speak at a board meeting or in front of the faculty, I was unprepared that he NEEDED me to go to France! Another teacher was unable to keep her chaperoning commitment and I was asked to travel with 15 young women to the City of Lights. Picking my jaw up from the floor, I quickly pulled out the suitcases. Since then, it's been a whirlwind of activity to prepare for my first international trip, my first trip across the ocean.

As I get ready to leave for Paris I'm reflective, wondering if I have everything I need. I do have the necessary clothes, toiletries and good walking shoes to tour the French countryside. I have the camera to capture all the incredible sites and experiences, and I have just enough money to buy something beautiful to treasure for years to come. What I don't know is if I have the brains, heart, and courage necessary to find my way back "home", to find my way back to myself.

This past week has been a storm of feelings. I've been moving through my days in slow motion as I re-live the events of the past six months. I felt cherished for the first time in my life and I'm not sure how to move away from that connection. Crowded with images of people and places as I try to find my footing, sleep is anything but welcome. When I awake and head out the door, I don't find the beauty of a life well lived, rather I'm confronted with my own inability to see all the colors of my life.

I once again made the mistake of traveling a path that was not mine. Part of me is so weary of this same journey, and I keep going in circles trying to find my heart; to find a place where it is safe. It seems like I have to keep learning the same lesson over and over again. The problem is, I have never quite figured out what the lesson is.

At my core I'm wired as a caretaker. Every career I considered: nursing, the Peace Corps, teaching, and social work are all in service to others. I'm not trying to rewire my basic psychological make-up. I AM trying to learn how to manage this never ending tendency to care more for others than for myself; to create a balance between loving and being loved. I should not need a passport to visit my own life. My life travels created a place where love is a constant and new adventures are just around the next bend. I've lost my way because I was walking a road paved by someone else. Somewhere during the last six months I let go of the very things that keep me grounded and I want them back.

What do I need to hang on to whether I am in a relationship or not? I need to get back my sense of adventure and my confidence. The many friends I've traveled this life with are still here and waiting. I need to look in the mirror and tell myself that I'm beautiful (and believe it) every day. I need to spend more time with my family. I need to ride my bike another hundred miles, go to the movies and laugh… a lot. I need to get tickets to see Toby and I need to clean my closets. I need to write my book and plant flowers. I need to buy new sheets. I need to meet my neighbors and walk the streets of my new neighborhood which I failed to do when I moved. I need to ride on Route 66 this summer and visit my sister's ranch. I need to dance, drink wine, and leave dishes in the sink. As much as I want to lock up my heart, I need to leave the key somewhere within reach.

On Thursday I leave for France, for Paris. Yes, I'm going to be responsible for the safety of 15 girls who are nervous to be traveling so far from home. I'm a teensy bit scared, but this trip is the perfect opportunity for me to start mending my broken heart. It is perfectly timed for me to take a break from the familiar landscape of my pain and re-discover my sense of wonder. I will stand in front of the Eiffel Tower and walk the beaches of Normandy. I will sit in a Parisian café and read a book. I will cry at the beauty of the countryside and be overwhelmed in the museums. Everything I see will be new, will be different. I will be different. And that is **exactly** what I need.

OLGA

From the moment I arrived at the airport, the number 15 was branded on my brain. Fifteen girls to get to Paris; 15 girls to get home. The next week meant constantly counting heads to ensure no one was left on the subway or the basement of a castle. It also meant experiencing the beauty and history of Northern France with 15 young women who soaked up the experience like sponges. We were guided on this adventure by Olga, a Russian born Paris educated woman, with tremendous spirit and an infectious smile that wrapped us all in warmth from the moment the plane touched down. Never did I expect how much she would teach me.

A petite brown-haired slip of a woman, Olga kept us all in line like ducklings with her bright red umbrella. One only needed to follow the colorful accessory held high above the crowds to know exactly where to head. For the first two days we walked Parisian streets via back alleys and subways, visiting the Eiffel Tower, Notre Dame, The Louvre, and Versailles. Tears flowed as I recalled photos of my father in front of the tower and felt his presence everywhere. We kept a hectic pace, with each moment being a stunning morsel of French culture. The Mona Lisa and Hall of Mirrors were exquisite examples of artistic genius and vanity. I was startled by the small size of the da Vinci masterpiece and figured out why Marie Antoinette was beheaded by her subjects. Through it all, Olga was a never ending source of information and energy!

Easter Sunday the group traveled to the village of Chartes to celebrate Mass in a centuries old cathedral that housed the veil of the Virgin Mother. During the two hour bus trip, Olga and I began to share tidbits of our own lives. She was the mother of a young son, looking to adopt a second child. Her love of languages found her asking me to interpret colloquial phrases she overhead from the girls. My love of asking questions found me eager to pick her brain on the history of the small towns and back roads. We found ourselves in easy conversation and banter, making the road time fly. Leaving Chartes, we headed out on a tour of royal estates that dotted the countryside.

The castles were stunning in their opulence and architecture. Detailed painted murals graced ceilings and intricately woven tapestries hung from the walls. Each housed a story of the marriages arranged for political gain and property. While all of that was good information, it was the story of the long suffering queens that had me enthralled and eager to know more.

Situated on the River Chen, sat the Chateau de Chenonceau, the home of King Henry II and Queen Catherine de Medici. Also sharing space was Henry's mistress and love of his life, Diana. Each woman had her own glorious garden, yet all I could think was, REALLY? Catherine had to actually live with her husband's lover? I was secretly thrilled when Olga shared that as King Henry lay dying, Catherine stripped his mistress of all her jewels and wealth, banishing her from the estate. Damn, I wish I could have done that three years ago! While 15 young women snoozed on the bus, Olga and I pondered the love lives of queens. Did they love their king, or did they perhaps, have their own secrets?

The next day, while visiting the amazing town of Saint Malo in the Brittany region of France, I discovered my new heroine, Queen Anna. Facing the English Channel, this historic town is surrounded by the walls of Anna's fortress. Now, this young child became a queen at the unlikely age of 12 when her father married her off to King Maximillian of Austria. The marriage was never consummated because the old guy was really too busy. When he failed to support Anna in battle, she took off and married King Charles VII of France, with the Pope validating the union. According to Olga, he died young after a racquetball accident! Anna did have a husband and, ultimately, was able to continue to rule Brittany on her own. She became my heroine because she didn't put up with the rules of the time and her personal motto was "I will never change". I LOVE that!

In San Malo, with the girls safely snug in their beds, the adults sat in a small café where Olga and I began to fantasize about writing a book about these queens; more specifically, about their love lives. Who did these women love? How did they cope with the rules and restrictions of the time? A glass of wine produced the title: "You Are Not My King, But I Love You". She would do the research, I would write the stories. Although exhausted by a day of walking, we were both energized as we discussed the possibility of collaboration.

As we traveled between villages, cathedrals, and castles, Olga and I continued to trade our own stories. These long bus rides provided lots of time for her to share glimpses of all things French and she loved learning of the intricacies of the English language.

Her quest for knowledge was infectious, and I wasn't at all surprised to learn she had studied for a summer at Oxford. I felt a growing bond that would remain even after we boarded the plane home.

For the remainder of the trip, it is not an understatement to say I wept my way across France. Each day seemed more amazing than the previous, and my senses were overwhelmed with the smells, sights, and tastes of the culture. The tour found us sampling snails in a cave, walking the brick paved streets of small villages, and being stunned by the sight of thousands of white crosses at Normandy. We ended the same place we started: Paris. A night time river cruise on the Seine left us in awe of the Eiffel Tower ablaze in lights.

Each day, at each stop, it was Olga who guided us through centuries of history and culture. Because of her, I did not lose even one of the 15 girls in my care. We were all touched by her wisdom and observations and there wasn't one among us who didn't have our photo taken with Olga on the last day. A long ride to the airport found us exchanging email addresses and committing to writing that book! I expected to be changed by this trip; I expected to come home with memories and souvenirs. Who knew that the best of those would come in the way of a new friend. I couldn't pack Olga away in my suitcase, but I am going to buy myself a red umbrella!

DREAM

During the years that her father lived in the Virgin Islands, Julie made several trips to visit him. She always returned with a trinket for me, and once included a special piece of jewelry. Known as an "island hook bracelet", it resembles a horseshoe on a thin silver band and is elegant in its simplicity. The legend of the bracelet is if worn with the open end facing the world you send the message your heart is open and looking for love. Worn with the hook facing your body indicates you have met your true love and your heart is taken. When Julie first presented me with the gift, I wore it every day. Gradually, I began to wear it less and actually misplaced it for a bit. Last night I had a dream that suggests I need to again make the bracelet a daily part of my wardrobe. Believe it or not, it was about Dorothy Gale…Dorothy of Oz fame.

In the dream Dorothy was, of course, trying to find her heart's desire. She was open to whoever might choose to travel the road with her. But this time, Dorothy had to accept the reality that the Scarecrow, Tin Man, and Lion were not friends she met to assist her on the journey, but were actually parts of herself that she had to accept in order to find her way home. At different points, Dorothy felt stupid, vulnerable, and scared. Until she saw herself as being smart, loving, and brave, she was doomed to wander the haunted woods for a very long time. I forced myself awake before Dorothy got hit with any more apples.

The images left me questioning my favorite movie character and my previous assumptions about her journey. I've always watched the flick with the belief that Dorothy needed the help of others to direct her travels. But what if Frank Baum's plan was to have us look inward and not outward? What if when he wrote the story, he wanted us, the reader, to examine our own strengths and the importance of determining our own path? Maybe "over the rainbow" wasn't about finding a better place, but about realizing that wherever we go, we take our true selves with us.

If it's true that our dreams are a reflection of our own struggles, then those are questions I need to answer. Why do I look more to others for my happiness and view myself as scared and stupid when it comes to love? The simple answer is, of course, that my heart has taken one too many hits and is wounded. The resulting damage leaves me vulnerable and unguarded. But the more complicated answer lies in figuring out why I'm drawn to people who don't want what I have to offer.

I've always found it easy to love and do so deeply. I believe, foolishly, that my love is strong enough to repair the damaged hearts of others. I get carried away with the idea that I can break through the walls of a heavily guarded castle and rescue the tortured soul. What I just don't seem to understand is that a heart rescued may not want to be, and just may not be a heart that can protect mine.

A wise colleague has suggested to me that this willingness to love without personal regard is both the best and the worst part of my personality. Risking having my heart broken is a natural consequence. My challenge is to learn to use my brains and strength to balance out the intensity of my emotions. It's a journey that has me weary because I seem to take the same number of steps backward as I do forward. I often wonder if this path is designed to keep me going in circles until I learn some lesson that I fail to see.

If you've read the book version of the *Wizard of Oz*, you know the Emerald City was so-named because, upon arrival, the travelers had to put on tinted glasses. I'm reminded that whatever Baum's intention was, the truth is, we only see what we want to see. If I don't clear my vision, I cannot possibly see the path in front of me. Maybe, if I stop searching so hard, whatever it is I am looking for will find me.

I woke up today and immediately put on that island bracelet. Yes, keeping my heart open sometimes takes more energy than I wish to invest. But to move through this life keeping my heart locked up…well, that's just plain cowardly.

DOORS

As a kid I loved the game show "Let's Make a Deal." The costumes and ridiculous possessions used by the contestants to get onto the show always made me giggle. I wanted to be model-assistant, Carol Merrill, and dress in beautiful clothes, and I wanted to kiss the host Monty Hall. What I loved the most was the risk that people took in believing that something better than what they had was perhaps, behind Door #2. I didn't realize then that contestants were most likely pre-selected or that winning might not have been random. I really didn't realize that the show was a good lesson in acceptance versus hope.

The memory popped up this weekend in, of all places, church. I've very recently re-discovered my love of the ritual of the Mass, even though I struggle with the politics of the church. The service always takes me back to the times in my life when I've felt safest and most loved. It also returns me to those moments when I've struggled and found peace in my faith.

Often, as I settle into the pew for my own private conversation with God, I may not even hear what's said on the altar. Yet this week, the homily struck a chord that resonated with me: it was about prayer. Since my trip to France, my go-to-girl for prayer has been Mary, the Mother of God. Viewing her veil in the Cathedral of Chartes moved my soul in a way I have rarely experienced. Not excluding the Big Guy by any means, I just find great comfort in this maternal figure. A Mary medal is a daily part of my wardrobe and I even find myself living in St. Mary's parish! I don't believe the trip to France, or living in this house, are coincidences in this faith journey.

Deacon Bob, a large bald man with just a hint of a beard, theorized that there are generally three responses that God has to our prayers: "No", "Yes", and "Wait", with the most common being "Wait". He went on to say that God does indeed want to answer our petitions, to give us what we desire. But as the faithful have been taught, responding to our requests comes on God's terms, not ours. Often, His way of answering our prayers is not to grant what we asked for, but it might just be what we need. I think one of the toughest parts of having faith is believing, that at any given moment, we are in the right place. That's when I began to think of "Let's Make a Deal." Can we accept where we are, what

149

we have, and not feel the need to trade up? Can we resist the urge to think something better is behind a door or curtain and not already in our hands?

When a door closes in our lives, the sound can be painful. If it's shut gently, we can hold on to the hope that it will again open. When it's slammed, we may find ourselves tempted to continue knocking, but we can only stand in front of it for so long before realizing it's never going to open. How long we stand there determines our ability to let go and move on.

I have spent too much time standing in front of one such door, hoping and praying it would open. How stupid. What a waste of my time. What a waste of my heart. Every once in a while, I would get a peek and think that what was behind the door was more valuable than what was on this side; I just had to be patient. I chose to believe that God was telling me to wait, when He was actually saying "No." Monty Hall was simply teasing me with the possibility of a great vacation when all that was really there was a giant plastic walleye, a smelly old fish. Not even the real thing. I'm angry with myself for believing in something that was never going to fulfill me. Unfortunately, it cost me more than having a set of nail clippers or a pomegranate in my purse, much like a contestant on the show. It cost me my self-confidence, faith, and pride in myself; way too high a price to pay and I want them back!

When doors stay closed it's because we're standing in front of the wrong one. God has already determined that, which is why it remains locked. We can pound all we want, but the truth is, until we move we can't even see there is another door...an open one. I don't know much, but I do know this: the prize is not on the other side. **I'm** the prize and I need to turn around because someone or something more worthy is waiting for me.

Forty years ago, Monty Hall gave people options. Keep what you can see or take a risk on what you can't. You might wind up with a new car or refrigerator, but you might just as likely wind up with a giant rocking chair. I don't think I'm going to try and make deals anymore. I think I'll just wait for God to show me the right door. When He does, it will open easily.

BLIND SPOTS

Beginning with my very first driving lesson, I was warned about the blind spot. You know the one: that spot just out of view of your car mirrors where danger lurks. The risk lies in attempting to change lanes, not seeing the oncoming car. There never seems to be a safe way to check if it's clear. I was trained not to trust the mirror and, if I turn my head, I take my eyes off the road. As cautious as I am, every once in a while I encounter the blare of a horn that signals I have, indeed, failed to notice impending trouble. Whenever this happens, I quickly send up a silent prayer to my guardian angels for once again saving my ass.

A recent conversation with a friend got me thinking about a different kind of blind spot, an emotional one. It's something that we know is never quite out of view, we can't always see coming, and need to confront repeatedly. No surprise that I forever feel chased by grief. From parental loss, to infertility, to the demise of my marriage, I've dealt with this ghost in multiple ways. Sometimes I heard a warning and other times I was blindsided. But, without a doubt, when I reflect on my losses I can see what I've gained.

With each loss in my life have come people and events to compensate. Yes, I felt cheated by Virginia's death, but my life has been filled with women who have nurtured and sustained me. I'm grateful beyond comprehension for those who have been mentors, cheerleaders, and confidantes; incredible women who challenge my thinking and yet always have my back. From them I have learned all I need to know about friendship and the value of jumping into a cold lake in December.

From the time of my first pregnancy, I knew to my core that I would never give birth. I can't say where this feeling came from, but even before ever getting pregnant, I knew. As I was making phone calls sharing my good news, a little voice kept whispering…"Don't say anything." I was never surprised by a miscarriage, never shocked. Although heartbroken each time, I somehow knew I would be a parent. Dad's phone call to me on that warm June afternoon telling me about Julie taught me to trust my instincts, even when I'm in doubt. I trust my own inner voices when others are telling me I'm traveling the wrong path. Until I hear a different one, I have to trust my own.

On the day I knew my marriage was finished, the

overwhelming feeling was one of fear. I envisioned myself as a lonely old woman with 14 cats, hiding behind my quilts and balls of yarn. Yet with the divorce came a sense of adventure that had previously been untapped. In the years since, I've gone white water rafting and zip lining, become a cyclist, scaled walls, and jumped over fire. My list of future adventures is long and limited only by my pocket book. I gained the knowledge that courage is more than facing fears: it is accepting that life is full of risks worth taking.

Losing Dad didn't occur in a blind spot, and despite the blaring horns, I didn't see driving into the wall of grief that was waiting for me. Last Father's Day found me struggling and, for some stupid reason, I didn't think the day would bother me. This year, I'm far more healed and I know to prepare for moments of sadness. Dad was, without a doubt, the most influential man in my life and grieving forced me to drive more defensively; to anticipate the unexpected.

Whether it's driving a car or loving others, I've had a few fender benders. Loving as deeply as I do, I'm not sure I want to see if there's something approaching. If I love with the idea that it will be lost, I can't fully embrace the potential that exists within any relationship. Loss may well be my emotional blind spot, but loving with my whole heart is the path I travel. There will be times my heart cannot avoid a collision. When that happens, I trust my guardian angels will tell me exactly which direction to head.

ENOUGH

When we were kids, Mom had to closely monitor our intake of sweets. The four of us, if left to our own devices, would have stuffed ourselves silly with Oreos or Ho-Hos. Mom kept the good stuff in a cabinet that only she could open. When Mom and Dad went out for an evening, it was not unusual for us to pool our change and head to the SuperX drug store for a bag of Brach's milk chocolate stars. One of us would trek to the corner carrying the precious $1.99. Upon return, we would count out the stars evenly and eat until we felt we had enough. Yet if offered more, we certainly would never have refused. We didn't need more treats, but boy did we want as much as we could get!

I often think of that "goodie cabinet" and how access seemed elusive. I have the same feeling when it comes to a healthy relationship. It always seems to be in view but just out of reach. I've learned to regulate my intake of sweets and forbidden foods, yet I seem to have more trouble when it comes to regulating what I want in this life and what I want from other people. I get very confused when trying to distinguish my wants from my needs, and I forever beat myself up for feeling needy.

For the last few years, I've been at constant war with myself about this very process. I'm too often willing to redefine myself and deny the very things I know will make my relationships work. Just this weekend, I again found myself willing to compromise to get what I want. Unfortunately, in doing so, I denied feeling fulfilled. I sent myself out for the chocolate stars and came back empty-handed.

I know this issue is deeply integrated into my personality and stems from a life history of loss and grief. I know it comes from a marriage steeped in dysfunction that significantly damaged my self-worth. Mostly I know that I'm exhausted from it all. I've had enough: enough of wanting what I can't have; enough of pretending my needs don't matter; enough of not accepting my life as is. Whatever my life is to be, wherever it is to take me, I do believe that today I'm exactly where I'm supposed to be.

As I continue to work on putting a collection of these random thoughts together in a book, I see the theme remains the same: I've blamed early losses, betrayal, and growing older for my unhappiness. I've lamented lost love and promised myself that I wouldn't close off my heart.

I've written more than one piece about working toward self-acceptance and living in the moment. I've reflected time and again about moving forward and personal growth. I've made promises not to compromise and to appreciate the gifts right in front of me. Yet in many ways, I haven't moved at all.

Close friends will disagree with that last statement. Had I stayed married, I'd have continued to be nothing more than wallpaper, watching life instead of living it. I'd have never embraced my new passions of cycling and writing, never developed the group of friends that nurture my soul, and never ever jumped into a freezing-ass cold lake! I've had more fun in the last six years than I had in the 20 years prior. But at my core, I continue to feel I'm lacking. I continue to feel that what will make me whole lies in someone else rather than recognizing my own strength and beauty. A dear friend recently told me (twice) that she knew no one who is as uncomfortable in their own skin as I am. Again, I say, "Enough!"

So here is where it ends. I'm done writing about lost love, dead parents, and missed opportunities. I'm done pontificating about lessons learned and daily struggles. I will no longer write about what is wrong in my life and what I feel is missing. I have filled pages with those thoughts and my editorial board has plenty of ramblings from which to choose. I've analyzed the movie, "Wizard of Oz", from every angle on the yellow brick road, and I've covered all the great emotions. I have challenges to yet confront but I can't think of one on which I haven't already reflected.

I will be writing about the people and events that cause me to embrace this life. I will continue to make observations on how life is really a collection of stories that make up a novel. I will be writing about the people I love and the gifts they bring. I will rejoice and celebrate anything that causes me to shed that uncomfortable skin and get back the swagger with which I was born.

Today I did many of my favorite things: I worked with my trainer, swam with my sister, and celebrated a good friend's new job success. I also went shopping for chocolate stars. I couldn't find any, as like many things from my past, they no longer exist. But this evening I'm going to curl up under a blanket with a large bowl of M and M's. I'll stop when I have had enough.

DRESS

My first memory of feeling beautiful in a dress was the day of my Confirmation. I wore a short sleeve A-line design with colored blocks of orange and cream. Falling just above the knee, it looked just fabulous with my fishnet stockings. I felt absolutely gorgeous until I saw a girl a few rows in front of me wearing the exact same frock…minus the fishnets. All I could think as we filed forward to receive our slap from the bishop, was that everyone would see HER first. I would walk up the aisle hearing the "tsks tsks" of every tongue in the church and I would feel their pity and disdain. Hours later, miserable, I gingerly hung the now ugly thing in my closet where it remained until it was donated or thrown out. Still, I remember that for a few moments that dress made me feel beautiful.

The next time I felt beautiful in that same church, was on my wedding day. On that occasion, no one else was wearing my gown, and this time the murmurs of "wow" and "oh my" were all around me. I spent the day feeling gorgeous and at the end of it all, I lovingly hung the flowing fabric in the wardrobe, until I had it preserved and sealed in a box. That container has been carefully moved many times in the last 28 years and I never opened it, fearful that exposure to air would ruin its fragile beauty. To me, the dress is an emotional reminder of the love and promise I felt on that day and a physical reminder of the vows I spoke.

Recently a wise person observed that even though I've been divorced for three years, I have yet to free myself from those vows. He went on to say that in many ways I've remained faithful to my commitment and that my belief in those words was keeping me closed off from new beginnings. It was a stinging realization of how tightly I hold on to the hope of the past. I let myself ponder those difficult words for a couple of weeks, deciding it was time to take a few steps forward; time to embrace the future and let go of the hurt. Time to do something about that dress.

Whenever I would open the closet door, the wrapped box loomed large, heavy with the weight of memories and fear of regrets. So many emotions tied up in that box. I hadn't seen the dress since I left it to be preserved and sealed; I couldn't even be sure if it was actually in there! I only knew one thing for certain: once removed, it was not going to return to the closet.

155

What was I going to do with it? One divorced friend told me she gave her wedding finery to Goodwill. Another suggested I burn the garment in a symbolic gesture to bury the memories. A happily married friend shared that she turned her dress into beautiful pillows for her bed. At one point, I considered having a christening gown made for Julie, but that ship has sailed. Sadly, Julie doesn't want to ever use the ivory threads herself. I thought of giving it to my sister for storage but quickly dismissed that idea as avoidance. Yet none of the other options seem to fit for my dress. I wanted to separate myself from the vows, but I didn't want to damage the memories.

As I began to share my dilemma with more friends and family, lots of plans were presented to me: have it made into a quilt; take it to a shop that sells used wedding gowns; donate it to an organization that sends dresses to women in Africa; give it to a local university theater program. Then came the perfect resolution....my sister-in-law, Laura, asked if she could use it as part of my Goddaughter, Madeline's, first communion dress. Wow! The significance of my gown being used by someone I adore for her own first walk down the aisle was a lovely, yet powerful thought. I was touched beyond words, knowing something beautiful could come out of this symbol of hope; it could be part of a big day for Madeline. It was the solution I had hoped for. With that, my perspective shifted. Up to that moment, I couldn't even imagine that I'd be able to take the box out of the closet by myself, let alone carry it to the car unassisted. But with this plan firmly set in mind, I found lifting the box easy, startled that it was not at all heavy.

Needing to shake the sealed container a bit to make sure something was indeed in it, I carefully began to cut away the protective wrapping. Lifting the lid and gently removing layers of tissue, I was surprised that I wasn't flooded with sadness. I was simply looking at a beautiful dress, a classic: ivory with a beaded bodice, pearled spaghetti straps, the layers of chiffon flowing gently from the empire waist. Tiny buttons held up the train, and a sheer jacket provided the necessary modesty required at the time. A coordinating headpiece completed the ensemble, and I noticed that both the dress and hat seemed to have shrunk! The majority of the fabric had indeed been preserved, even though I noticed a bit of yellowing on the buttons and on the edges of the bodice. But the anticipated overwhelming rush of emotions had not occurred! Opening the box had not brought me to my knees. Opening the box had elevated my heart.

The tough part over, it was time to take the dress to Laura and my young niece. Madeline came running from the other room, excited to see what would soon be part of her special day. She cautiously opened the lid and immediately took possession of the hat and popped it on her head. Next came the requisite "oohs and aahs", and the fabric was viewed with a critical eye toward the possibilities. Madeline, done with the excitement of it all, retreated to the couch with a book. Still wearing the hat, veil over her face, she was the epitome of grace and charm. It was one of those small moments of joy that so often get overlooked, but suddenly I could see it clearly. Because in that instant, I knew that it wasn't about where the dress had been or what it meant. It was about what it could become. Actually, it was about what **I** could become. The dress held no power. It had no hold on my heart. It was simply a reminder of a time when I felt loved, beautiful, and adored. It has been suggested to me that those are feelings I want to remember because when I feel them again, I will both recognize and reach for them.

Madeline is just beginning a journey that will include a million beautiful dresses. At the end of the day, when HER dress is hanging in HER closet, I will have taken a huge step along my own path. I think I'll look for something in orange and cream to wear.

NAME

When I got married, the expectation was very clear: if I give birth, the child's first name would start with the letter J. My husband and each of his brothers had a first name with that consonant and the family tradition was to continue. I simply smiled and privately thought I would comply when hell froze over. But Julie was such a surprise that, in the moment, it seemed like a small issue. Had I been given a choice, I would have named her Lauren or Catherine or Diane. She was horrified by those choices, as she always saw herself as more of a Claire or Sophia. If given an opportunity, she'd have changed her name in a hot minute.

Growing up, I had a similar feeling about my name. Susan was okay, although everyone called me Sue. I hated my middle name, Jean. I hated it because everyone else in my family had Ann as a middle name. Each of my sisters, my mother, all had Ann somewhere in their name. I get that Susan Ann made no sense, but Jean? If I could suggest a do-over, I would pick Lynn or Elizabeth. Susan Marie has a nice ring to it.

Somewhere in my 20's, I preferred to be called Susan and began to introduce myself as such. 30+ years later, some members of my family still call me Sue, which for the most part, I accept. There is an even smaller circle of individuals who can get away with calling me Susie: one is 84 years old, and the others have special permission based on history or intimate knowledge of my soul. There's a niece and a couple of nephews who have given me the nickname, Aunt Sue-Bird, which I find charming. To everyone else, I'm Susan.

I come by this name conflict honestly. Dad hated his given name, Myron. He often told me the story of how his mother looked around the room after his birth, and her eyes landed on the doctor who bore the same name. His twin sister, born just a few moments later, was graced with the most holy of names, Mary, and he was stuck with Myron. Dad was always referred to as Mike, and I never heard him use his given name. He signed all documents as M. H. Emmerich, and that's how it appeared on my wedding invitations.

I never hesitated taking my husband's surname. It was the 80's, women's lib was a bit stalled, and I wanted to be identified as a couple...as a "Mrs." It was also a golden opportunity to ditch Jean and use Emmerich as my middle name. It seemed the perfect way to remain loyal to my roots while embracing my future. When the marriage ended, it didn't occur to me to change back. My married name had a nice ring to it, and I had a professional history linked to it. I also wanted to remain connected to Julie by sharing the same surname.

The thought of returning to Emmerich began to slowly enter my psyche when Dad passed. I remember sitting in the funeral home, listening to how the obituary would read, thinking that I wanted to be listed as Susan Emmerich. I brushed the thought aside as a grief response and for the next year, paid no attention to the continuing little pricks to my brain. When I allowed them to linger for even a few seconds, I reminded myself of how much work would be involved.

At the same time I was grieving Dad, I was also taking the first major steps in finally separating emotionally from my marriage. The divorce was well behind me but I was far from done. Both were painful processes with a lot of emotional overlap. When I was being honest with myself, those brain pricks were more about my anger and less about my grief. If I were going to take this step, it needed to be for the right reasons and not just an emotional reaction. So I began to think about who I wanted to be for the remainder of my days. Moving forward, what did I want to be called? No matter how many ways I asked the question, the answer kept coming up the same...Susan Emmerich.

Still, I felt the need to check this decision with a few folks. I started with Julie. In typical Julie fashion, she simply looked at me and said, "Why would it make a difference to ME? It's your name. I'm not keeping it forever." I then began to verbalize the idea to my inner circle. With few exceptions, the response was the same: "Why wouldn't you do it?" or, "What's taken you so long?" The only remaining challenge was timing.

Today is Thursday, May 9th. Dad's birthday. Today is the perfect day to file for a name change and honor my father. I'll smile as I file the documents and remember his life. Yes, it's going to be a paperwork hassle. Yes, it's going to be annoying to change my driver's license and social security card. Those are temporary inconveniences. In the end, it's about continuing to define myself on my terms, and to recognize that where I'm headed is rooted in where I've been. Just to be perfectly clear…Jean is not coming with me.

WASHSTONE

Julie was just 2 years old the first time I took her to Washstone, my sister's ranch in western Massachusetts. Pictures of her perched on a horse with her cousin, Greg, and another of them happily eating dirt, are stored in a large plastic container in the hall closet. It was the beginning of a wonderful annual tradition and Julie now has countless memories of summer trips there. I have my own mental snapshots of her and her cousins swimming in the river, harvesting frogs from the pond, and chasing turkeys out of the house. Julie took an annual "first" riding lesson at least five times and my niece Danielle, only 12, loved driving us around on 4-wheelers. Traveling to the ranch meant long afternoons sunning myself on the deck, reading two novels a week and hiking through the pines on the back 40. I will never forget the infamous night of camping that's memorable for a leaky tent, deflating air mattress, and panting dog. What is most branded on my brain is the knowledge that Washstone has always been the best place for me to re-discover what grounds me.

I spent this past weekend visiting Nancy for her 60th birthday celebration, which was arranged by Danielle. I had my nails done, drank and ate a bit too much, shot rifles in the sand pit and saw a newborn calf take its first step. I was brave enough to finally walk a horse to the barn and was ready to get serious about conquering my fear of riding; I discovered I'm less cautious while wearing a good pair of farm boots and old jeans.

Over the past 20 years, only Julie and I visited the ranch; her father chose not to accompany us. The last few years I have mostly gone alone. This time, my two brothers were also along, and there were lots of opportunities to laugh and be ridiculous. Each of us surprised Nancy at a different time and so the energy level stayed high. Neither of the brothers had visited in years and never had we been there together. As we took in all the activity that is the life of this place, I felt I was learning some aspects of the ranch for the first time. But something felt different; something was shifting.

On the surface, the ranch looked the same. There were some new chickens, the same stream of riders through the barn, and the same rhythm to the day. Nancy and Lee still rise early to do chores and Greg and Danielle continue to have their own projects. There's always a gate to be closed, a boarder to pacify, or a fence to be repaired. But something was "new" and it wasn't until the flight home that the thoughts began to settle. There was an ever growing sense that the ranch is about more than horses and chickens; about more than tractors and hay. It's about being grounded to something, someplace, or someone. Nancy and Lee are the life of Washstone and Greg and Danielle have added their own sweat and toil. All of them breathe the life of the ranch and it's what sustains them. Prior to this visit, I always viewed Washstone as their job; their home. During this visit, I began to view the ranch as the people who live there and not as the chores they do. This place connects them not only to the land but to each other. Whatever struggles come their way, each of them knows they are forever bound by a life shared.

That's been missing for me for the last year, maybe since just after Dad passed. I've been desperately seeking someone to share what is left of this life or at least to share parts of it. Yet the reality is, at this age it's harder to merge lives, to merge histories. I have a life that I don't want to abandon for someone else and I can't imagine anyone wanting to do that for me. As a young bride, it was an easy decision and a natural process. Now I don't think it can be done in the same way and I struggle with figuring out how to do it.

I know the window closed on my being able to build my own Washstone when my marriage ended. But being with my family this weekend reminded me that I'm still tied to something bigger than myself. Having family come together to celebrate Nancy made my heart sing for the first time in months and I realized I've been ignoring connections that already exist. Anyone who enters my world now will be woven into the fabric of my life story.

As I watched that newborn calf take its first shaky steps, I knew exactly how she felt. Yes, this life is an ever shifting landscape and yes, sometimes it actually quakes. The calf got up and fell down more than once, but before too long she was standing alone just fine. I'm sure that by today, she's already running.

PAWS

Last week, while SWIMMING, I had a hot flash! I was surprised by the heat that rushed to my face, while submerged in COLD water! Chalking it up to a natural physical reaction, I laughed my way through the remaining laps. I've experienced these occasional flashes for a couple of years, struggled with periodic insomnia, and every once in a while felt a bit cranky. I assumed I was cruising through menopause with minimal problems, just like other female relatives. But since when has my body reacted as anticipated?

I'm beginning to believe that perhaps this transition isn't going as smoothly as I hoped, as my moods are all over the place. I can move through the entire emotional spectrum in less than 45 seconds. Being alone in my car is like the ending of the movie "Beaches"; I find myself weeping to and from work. One day a colleague called me out for my snap response to a simple question. Tears began to cascade down my face and five minutes later I was laughing. Feeling crazy is a new experience and I've been assuming this mess of reactions is related to a change IN my life rather than the change OF life. Recognizing this possibility has brought some clarity to the situation and opened up the door to potential remedies. Herbal supplements (of the legal kind) have brought some relief and today, for the first time in months, I felt something I almost didn't recognize. Funny, I owe it to a tiny little dog in the park.

After three days in meetings with 200 other college counselors, I needed to clear my head. The conference was great and I saw many of my favorite colleagues from around the state. I ate and drank too much and had no time for exercise. When I arrived home this afternoon the sun was shining and I needed to move! I was cautious about a solo ride because the last time I pedaled alone I ended up with a flat tire. Cycling is the best way for me to regain my equilibrium and so, after a quick tire inspection, I set off for the bike path. My intent was to do an easy 10 miles and take in the sounds and smells of early summer, yet my legs felt heavy and I wondered if I could make it to the 5 mile turnaround point.

I almost fell off my bike when the little "purse dog" came into view. A young woman had the miniature pup on a leash and was standing just off the path. With all four paws firmly planted on the ground, this miniature dog was pulling hard on a leash in its mouth. The other end was attached to a Saint Bernard! I swear that little critter was smiling with perseverance and determination. The large dog, on the other end of that leash, was just standing, oblivious to the hard work of his friend. Stopping, I dismounted and took a moment to pet them both. For the first time in months, I actually felt my heart smile and felt an unfamiliar sensation. A feeling I didn't recognize...hope.

Back on my bike, my legs felt stronger and the miles began to melt away. I passed the 5-mile turnaround and kept going when I saw a young cyclist weaving along the trail. The tongue between his teeth told me he was new to a bike with no training wheels. A mile later, the 80-year old guy wearing a speedo walking through the field was a startling vision, but his strut told me he felt confident. When I reached the 10-mile mark, I chatted with a man much older than I, who was turning around after 15. We rode together for a few moments, chatting about the perfect weather before he sped ahead. It seemed today was going to be about meeting dogs and people who were pushing past what others might expect of them. None of them were giving in to perceived limits and were simply enjoying the day.

It's been a long time since a bike ride was as cathartic as this one. Approaching my driveway, I noticed 20 miles were recorded on my odometer. More importantly, a sense of hope was recorded on my heart. I'm weary of this "change" impacting my life so dramatically. I'm exhausted that this roller coaster of emotions determines how I spend my day. I'm particularly fed up with feeling like I have no choice. Yes, my body chemistry is shifting, and yes, I need to develop some strategies for managing the process, but I don't have to give in to it!

I'm going to channel my inner "little dog." I'm going to grab that leash and pull with all my might. When I feel off balance I'm going to stick out my tongue and hold on. When I feel like my body is failing me, I'm going to think of the fine old man in the speedo. To train for the century, I'm going to regularly push myself to ride five more miles than I intend.

No way is the roller coaster ride over. I know that. Tonight I'll push the covers off as frequently as I pull them on, but will be grateful I can reach out and open the window to let in a cool breeze. I'll cry when I should laugh but will remind myself that tears wash away bad feelings to make room for good ones to grow. I will have moments when I feel discouraged but I'll remember that

today I felt normal. Today my heart smiled. Today that is enough.
Even if I'm hot.

JEWEL

In May, Julie gave me a wonderful Mother's Day gift. She drained her bank account to buy two tickets to see Toby Keith. Now, as great as seeing Toby will be, the true gift is that Julie is going with me. I was actually incredulous that she is choosing to experience my favorite performer in the seat next to mine, particularly since she regularly makes fun of my passion for Toby. No doubt, I've received some great gifts in my time: my first bicycle, a writing journal, an old quilt. All have led to my passions of riding, writing, and quilting. But my greatest passion has been the privilege of being Julie's mom. Today, June 16th, I'm reminded that of all the gifts I've received over the years, Julie is the most cherished.

Julie, who became my baby, turns 21 today. Unbelievable. The memories of those first early days in South Dakota are branded on my soul. I didn't give birth, but I did go through labor for 24 hours. It started with begging the airline agent for a ticket, continued with promising Lori I would love this child, and finally concluded with a trip to Kmart for two cartloads of baby "stuff." When I walked out of the hospital the next day with Julie, she did not yet have a name. But she did have my heart.

Those early days in Mitchell were spent like many first days between mothers and infants. I struggled with getting her to take a bottle, understanding her cries, and getting some sleep. I had to adjust her formula, change diapers, and became a fan of David Letterman. Julie's allergic reaction brought an early lesson in parental fear and anxiety, feelings that are now old friends. By the time we returned home, Julie and I had already written the first several chapters of our shared story. In the 21 years since, our time together has created a novel. Some chapters stand out more clearly than others.

A nightly bath routine always included wrapping Jules up in a towel and singing Beatles' songs in her ear. By the time she was 18 months old, Julie could belt out a version of "All My Loving" that would win a karaoke contest. My favorite Herman's Hermits song still resonates in her brain, and her love of music was born out of my off- tune renditions. Often were the nights that Julie and I would snuggle in her bed reading book after book. We read the entire *Little House on the Prairie* series, as well as the *Chronicles of*

Narnia. On the nights she couldn't fall asleep, Julie would ask to "listen to my heart" until she dozed off on my chest. Never once did I deny that request. Nor did I ever fail to recognize those shared moments as irreplaceable.

I can't claim credit for Julie's beauty or eye color, but I will say she gets her love of asking questions directly from me! It seems like yesterday that Julie was digging for worms in the front yard and found some bones. Ever curious, she examined her discovery with great interest and was adamant in her desire to know exactly what pre-historic creature she had unearthed. We packed them up and headed to the Natural History Museum to share her treasure with an archeologist. Barely maintaining his composure, he announced to the young explorer that she had dug up chicken bones, most likely buried by a neighborhood raccoon. Jules hadn't discovered the remains of some mythical beast, but she did discover that one needs only to go looking in the front yard to find adventure.

I never lied to Jules about the details of her birth or withheld any information. Multiple children's books about adoption lined her bookshelf, and I made it clear that she was loved by many people. I never picked up on any conflicts until that day in the park, that day she didn't want to leave when it was time for dinner. As I made my way down the path, still in view, Julie, aged 7, climbed to the very top of the jungle gym and yelled: "Well, if you're gonna leave me in a park, I don't know why you bothered to adopt me!" I paused only momentarily to gather my composure, but I knew in that instant that far more was going on in her pretty little head than she would let me know. Whatever questions she entertained, she kept to herself until she was ready to go searching on her own. Her need for answers was her journey. That is, until the time came to meet her birth family. It was the instant I knew what it meant to love without concern for my feelings. It was the moment I knew that despite where life might take Julie, we were indeed bonded.

This young woman has never once disappointed me. Oh, we have argued and we have disagreed and she's always stealing my socks. Jules has changed her hair color more than I've changed dress sizes, and don't get me started on her tattoos! She's allowed me to comfort her, forced me to challenge her, and taught me the value of silence. I've wept when Julie is sad and rejoiced when she succeeds. I have simultaneously wanted to strangle and embrace her. In short, I've been her mother.

Twenty-one years ago, I spent my first sleepless night as a parent in my father's South Dakota home. For the last 7,670 days, I haven't fallen asleep without saying a prayer for Julie. Every night I recite the same prayer: "Dear Lord, please guide and protect this child. May her joys outweigh her sorrows and may she know this day that she is strong, she is smart, and she is beautiful."

Realistically, I know I'll spend less time with Julie in the future than I have to this point. She now needs me in a different way. That's the reality of being a parent. But on July 19th, Julie is taking me to see Toby. She's excited because she can have a beer. I'm excited because it will be my fifth Toby concert. But it will be the first Toby show at which the person in the adjoining seat makes me happier than the person on stage. I think I'll spring for the premium parking.

CRUMBS

On a warm day in May, I fell in love with the city of Portland, Oregon. Forget that it's visually stunning, has miles of biking trails, or is home to VooDoo Donuts. I fell in love with Powell Books, a one square block, 3-story bookstore that I wandered through for hours. Tucked in the back, I found a small journal style book that asks a different thought provoking question each day. Is that perfect for me or what? It's set up as a 5- year record of random thoughts, so that on this day next year, I answer the same question and see what's changed. Over the past few weeks, the prompts have ranged from: "Write the first sentence of your autobiography" to "If your mood were a weather forecast, you'd be…" Some days, my responses have been immediate, and on others, I've pondered it throughout the day and written my answer later.

Yet, none of the questions has had me reflecting as much as one that came from my sister, Barbie. It was a random text that said: "Please explain how silverware dividers get so dirty if all you put in them is CLEAN silverware." I nearly fell out of my office chair laughing, as I quickly thought of my own need to clean the kitchen drawers. Understanding that a possible answer is that crumbs fall on the counter and then get brushed into the drawer, I came to realize the far reaching implications of her observation.

I have a history of being fairly organized and neat. Each year since my divorce, I've become a little less OCD. I have found there are far better uses of my Saturday mornings than ALWAYS cleaning the house. There are bike rides and meeting friends for tea, lounging in bed with the paper, and watching my niece play basketball. Singing in the shower beats cleaning the shower every time. I'll never let things get so out of control that I'm embarrassed to let someone in the front door, but there are times I would never let that same visitor open a closet or look under the bed!

The bigger question is: how, if we're living a good life and following the rules, do things get so messy? Why is it we never see the crumbs until they have accumulated to the point of needing to be removed? I don't see the dirt in the silverware drawer on a daily basis, only when it looks disgusting. How did I miss what was obviously collecting all along?

The simple answer, trite as it sounds, is "Because." Because life, at its core, is messy. Because our lives are complicated by emotions and relationships and those cannot be divided like the forks and knives. They're not separate and distinct but a constantly revolving collection of needs that bump into each other. They rarely nest together in a neat pile and none of us gets out of this life without spills and breaks. But we can learn how to clean up the mess before it gets overwhelming. It's a matter of how we choose to frame the problem.

For some reason, when we're struggling, we quickly forget the times when our lives were easier, or at least smoother. All we can see is the problem in front of us. That's the moment when the crumbs sneak into the drawer. Taking advantage of our distraction, they slowly pile up, slightly out of sight, until we pay attention; until we stop focusing on our own misery and look beneath the surface.

We don't know fear if we haven't felt safe. We can't know anger if we haven't previously felt peace. How do we know we feel sick if we haven't had days of good health? Anxiety doesn't come without acceptance. We certainly don't grieve if we have not loved.

I love starting my day with the silly question from my new journal, such as: "Water, ice or steam?" What I love more is how I'm choosing to end my day. In the same journal, there's enough room to also record something good that happened that day: the movie that made me laugh, happy hour with friends, a walk with Julie, or a good workout are all daily opportunities to feel joy. Those small events add up over time and can balance out the struggles.

I don't have an answer to Barbie's question. It's a dilemma well known to us all. I do know that at the end of the day, we do not get crumbs unless we have eaten cake.

PAPPY

In over 25 visits to Washstone Ranch, I have carefully studied the horses and been captivated by their beauty and intelligence. I've grown fascinated with the psychology of the herd and love knowing that if it includes a mare, she's the one in charge. I've observed the unique differences in their personalities, marveled at their relationships, and felt intimidated by their power. I relish the moments when I hear the sound of their collective gallop and fantasize about riding across a hay field atop a running stallion. Yet, in all these visits, I've never been on the back of a horse, never trotted around the riding ring sitting in a saddle. Never. Ever. As beautiful as these creatures are, they scare the hell out of me.

This past weekend brought an unexpected opportunity to go visit Nancy and Lee, and I decided to ride. I informed my sister of this desire and made it clear that I didn't consider having one of the 13-year old barn girls leading me around the indoor ring, as "riding." Nancy made it clear that she was going to treat me as a beginning riding student and teach me about horses. Little did I know how much I would learn about myself in the process.

When the time arrived for my lesson, I headed to the barn in borrowed jeans and farm boots, expecting the horse to be saddled and ready for me to mount. Instead, Nancy introduced me to Pappy, a beautiful Appaloosa who needed to be groomed before being saddled up. She then added that I was to do the grooming! First came the curry brushing to loosen the dirt in his coat, the hard brushing to remove the dirt, and the soft brushing to smooth it all back. I learned how to get Pappy to lift his hoof so I could clean the bottom of his feet and remove any debris. Imagine…ME, lifting the leg of a horse to clean his toes! Rarely have I even cleaned stalls, let alone the bottom of a horse's hooves. Any fears of getting kicked in the head were unnecessary, as Pappy was most compliant.

To me, this whole routine seemed odd. I likened it to showering before going jogging and didn't quite get the reasoning. Nancy gave me a look that could kill and simply said: "You are spending time with your horse before you ask him to work for you." It was less about the grooming and more about relationship building. She taught me I needed to let the horse know I was present, to feel comfortable with each other. Hmmm.

I will gloss over details of saddling up Pappy, as there were movements so smoothly and quickly made by my sister that I couldn't grasp the process. I was in awe of her ability to instinctively know the complicated steps that secured the saddle to the horse. In no time, my foot was in the stirrup, and I was swinging my leg up and over the saddle (a task made much easier with the help of a mounting block). It felt unnatural, awkward, and scary. My admiration for my niece, Danielle, grew a thousand fold as I remembered watching her at horse shows, jumping horizontal poles at a fast clip. I was sure that as soon as Pappy took a step, I would tumble to the ground.

As my sister barked out orders, I learned the basics of directing the horse. Sit up straight. Settle into the saddle. Lean back and keep my heels down. The reins were for communicating, not for holding on. If I wanted Pappy to go right, I needed to apply pressure on the left and open up the right rein. The reasoning is that horses instinctively move away from pressure. Wow, how smart are they? The opposite was true if I wanted Pappy to go to the left. "Walk" and "Whoa" were words Pappy understood, and I better not make a kissing sound or he would break into a gallop! I quickly learned that horses can, and do, sense if the rider knows what they're doing. My inexperience was obvious and it wasn't long before Pappy began to wander where he wanted to go until I was able to take charge and direct his pattern. So it was with only a rudimentary beginning that Nancy, Danielle, and I headed out for a trail ride.

Pappy navigated the familiar route easily, making me feel less nervous in my limited riding skills. I've always found great peace and beauty in the property that Lee and Nancy have so lovingly safeguarded for over 20 years. Atop Pappy, the view was spectacular! We rode a path I've walked many times and saw sights I hadn't previously. The hay field appeared almost majestic from up high and the pine woods have a serenity on horseback I haven't felt on foot. When Pappy lost his footing for less than a second, I kept my head and didn't panic. Actually, it felt as if I were about to be propelled over his head, but Danielle assured me my ass never left the saddle!

I quickly understood how riding could become addictive and I felt something shift inside me. For years I felt intimidated by the idea of riding, but on this day, I ignored those old feelings and took a chance. I felt brave. I felt strong. I never would've guessed that a horseback ride would also be a lesson in life skills. Nancy taught me that one of the first things a horse needs to learn is patience. Danielle taught me that horses instinctively move away from pressure. Pappy taught me to trust my ability to take control. Quite a riding lesson. I think the next time, I'm going to trot!

FAITH

One of my favorite quotations is: "Hope is the ability to hear the music of the future. Faith is being willing to dance to it today." I have absolutely no idea who to credit for these wise words but they hang in both my office and on my refrigerator. They're a reminder that having hope and faith make the daily trials of this life just a wee bit easier. My own faith journey has had more than one detour over the years, and my trip to France and my niece, Megan, have caused it to be renewed.

The beauty and power of the French Cathedrals were overwhelming; each one more breathtaking than the last, and I could feel the centuries of prayers that had been offered. No place was that feeling more intense than in the Cathedral of Chartres where we celebrated Easter Mass. Hundreds of years old, the church was stunning in its architecture, stonework, and stained glass. The Mass was equally stunning in its simplicity and although I didn't understand a word, the familiar ritual fit like an old pair of jeans (which was good since it was freezing). I felt God's presence in those stone pews and, more importantly, in my heart where there has been a hole. Good fortune had taken me to Chartres; I now believe it was so I could find my soul. You see, it was there, in this small town in Northern France, that I re-discovered my faith and where I came to know Mary.

In a small corner of this magnificent church, a thousand plus year old piece of the Virgin Mother's veil is on display. Encased in an intricate gold frame and locked behind a brass gate, the ancient fabric can be viewed. Rows of candles line the borders of the alcove and can be lit in prayer by the faithful. The silence was deafening and tears rolled down my cheeks as I knelt in prayer and lit a flame in thanksgiving for all my blessings. It didn't matter if I could cognitively accept that this relic had existed thousands of years ago, it mattered only that I believed.

For the next six days I searched for Mary medals as reminders of that moment in Chartres. I kept coming up empty-handed; even the fifteen students with whom I traveled were keeping an eagle eye out for simple medallions. Ever the great tour guide, Olga, kept trying to figure out how to get us back to a special shop in Paris where such medals were plentiful, but we never got there. I boarded the plane empty-handed, but with a sense that I'd actually found something that was missing, a focus for my prayers. More specifically, to whom I would pray: Mary. It was she who took the greatest leap of faith and it was she who ordered Jesus to perform his first miracle. I mean, this woman how knew how to get things done! Weeks later, I was over-the-moon delighted when a package of Mary medals arrived from Paris, a gift from Olga. I wear mine daily and started to recite the Hail Mary as my mantra. I immediately gave one to each of the students on the trip and to all the important women in my life. One of those women is Megan.

I remember well the night of her birth. It was Super Bowl Sunday, 1982. My roommate and I were busy preparing food for a party when the phone rang. My sister Barbie was in labor. I stayed focused on the Cheese Whiz while I waited for news which arrived just before half time. Megan was born and everyone was healthy. A quick phone call with Dad arranged our visit to the hospital at the end of the game, to get an early peak at the first Emmerich grandchild. My dad, with a tear in his eye, looked at Megan and remarked on her beauty. To Dad, Megan was special. Not just because she was the first, but because of the joy she brings to all who meet her.

As a toddler, I once dropped Megan on her head. We were doing flips in the living room, and I lost my grip as she climbed my legs. My brother-in-law didn't talk to me for two weeks. But Megan and I already had a special relationship and he eventually let me babysit again. I fondly recall the times I would take Megan to church. Arriving at her house, I watched her bound down the front steps in a white sailor dress with a head full of curls bobbing away. Walking hand in hand we entered church, knelt side by side, and went to communion. Breakfast at IHop always followed and I loved pretending she was my daughter.

My head is filled with special memories: staying with me the night her sister was born; the picture of her laying in the pew on my wedding day; making her jumpers and quilts as Christmas presents; Megan and her sister, Bridget, visiting me in Pennsylvania. When we returned to Cleveland, it was Megan who was Julie's babysitter and confirmation sponsor. I've been blessed to watch her grow from a precocious toddler to an amazing young woman. I'm not exaggerating when I say "amazing." Megan has told me on more than one occasion, that she greatly respects how I've handled adversity. I always just shake my head, surprised by her view. The reality is, I have much to learn from her and how she moves through this world with compassion, grace, and acceptance.

We were having dinner this week to catch up on our lives. I have to admit, I'm fortunate my nieces and nephews still enjoy spending time with their "old aunt." We shared pasta and wine as we complained about the struggles of being educators and the challenges of relationships. I was startled by the similarities, despite the almost 30 year age difference, and was struck by how much more wisdom Megan seemed to have then I did at that same age. I'm forever impressed with how she has handled difficult situations. She's no longer a little girl or adolescent, she's a grown woman of intelligence and insight. During dinner, one word kept coming to mind, one word that defines her essence: faith. Megan's unwavering commitment that she's guided in this life by God is overwhelming. I was impressed with how she believes to her core that she's in the right place, even if she doesn't always like the view, and trusts the right path will be presented to her. That's what faith is about: believing the path we travel is the right one even when it is tough. The Virgin Mary believed and so does Megan. They've each taught me that with faith comes clarity; with clarity comes acceptance.

Our faith wanes at times. If it didn't, we wouldn't need it. When I feel frustrated and fed up I'm going to reach for the medal that hangs around my neck. I'm going to remember that moment of awe in a beautiful French Cathedral and I'm going to recall that curly- haired toddler jumping in my car to attend mass. I like to believe those trips to church contributed to Megan's faith journey. I know for certain that she's presently contributing to mine.

GIRLS

At Julie's 6th birthday party, she received a Barbie doll. She politely thanked the gift giver and put the doll aside. Later, she looked at the gift with a puzzled expression and simply said, "What is that?" It was one of my proudest parenting moments, as I felt I'd accomplished a great feat in getting Julie through six years of life without ever playing Barbie! I wanted desperately to raise her believing she was more than a "girl." I wanted her more focused on what she could do, rather than how she looked. An incident this past week proved that while Julie does not feel limited by her gender, I seem to be the one embracing a Barbie mentality.

The scuffling noise coming from the laundry area caused both the dog and me to sit straight up in bed. I laid back down thinking perhaps I'd imagined the noise. It was, after all, 4:00 in the morning. But just to be sure, I called out Julie's name, thinking she might be in the kitchen. When she didn't answer, I rolled over, convinced it was just the sounds of the night. But then I heard it again. This time there was no mistaking the realization that something was in the house!

I ruled out the idea of a human intruder and recalled a friend's recent experience finding a mouse in her washing machine. I wondered if there were indeed a little critter scrambling to get out. Realizing the washer lid was open, I got out of bed prepared to take a peek inside the machine and slam the lid shut. I even had thoughts of turning on the Maytag to drown the damn thing! Switching on the hall light, I cautiously peered down into the washer and was relieved to see nothing but the empty drum.

Breathing a sigh of relief, I raised my head only to come face to face with the culprit! The beady little eyes and long pointy snout staring at me from a distance of only nine inches made it clear that I was not alone! Hissing and perched on the edge of the lid (actually on top of my favorite cycling jersey), sat an opossum! Yes, you read that right, an OPOSSUM!!!

What happened next can best be described by remembering Macaulay Culkin in "Home Alone!" Throwing my hands over my face, I screamed and stumbled backwards. Running down the hall to Julie's room, I had only one thought: "I am a GIRL." I don't know or care what a piston is, I can't change a tire, and I really really don't want to deal with wild animals in the house! Still screaming bloody murder and feeling that the huge creature was right behind me, I flew into Julie's room terrified for my life!

Completely freaked out by my entrance, Julie and I stood in her room screaming at each other. Convinced I was being chased by a masked gunman, Julie couldn't believe I was hysterical about an opossum. Gathering her wits, my brave daughter went to assess the situation. She found the disgusting creature still perched in the exact same spot. I, on the other hand, put the dog outside and locked myself in the bathroom.

If you know Julie, you know that in another life she was the original Dr. Doolittle. Her first thought was to speak softly and express delight! I could hear her laughing, trying to convince me how cute "Oliver" was. Seriously? She was making friends and naming the rabid invader? Through the bathroom door I continued to shout directives: "Find some gloves. Throw a towel over it! Kill it with a broom! GET RID OF IT!!" Instead, she got a carrot, convinced she could entice it to follow her out of the house. Unsuccessful and donning a pair of gloves, Julie then reached to pick up the critter. He responded by jumping behind the dryer, curling up, and playing dead in the corner. Great.

Being the adult in this family, I decided I needed to take charge: I called the police. Begging the dispatcher to help me, I clarified that I was a GIRL living alone with my daughter and had no resources to deal with this critical situation. Laughing, she said the sergeant agreed to send a car and, within two minutes, a GUY was here to handle this crisis. Although of only average size, he appeared incredibly brave and confident with his badge and gun. I let him in the front door, and returned to my safe space in the bathroom. Julie assisted him in pulling out the dryer to find "Oliver" tightly entrenched in his corner. The first officer on the scene then called for back-up.

With two more men in blue in the laundry room, attempts to sweep Oliver into a dust pan proved futile and finally—according to Julie—one of the officers simply picked him up by his tail and carried him outside. Julie also observed, this huge menace, was no bigger than a shoe. He must have shrunk since the time we shared eye contact, because in my mind, this rodent was the size of our cocker spaniel! I hugged Julie, relieved that we were both alive and more than a little impressed with her confidence and bravery. She just shook her head and got into the shower.

As I cleaned the dust from behind the dryer and returned things to their proper place, I couldn't help but feel a bit ridiculous. I've spent years teaching Julie to feel confident and strong. I've worked tirelessly to role model those attributes and to rely on my own resources. I can bounce back from emotional distress better than anyone I know, but going nose to nose with a BABY opossum caused me to dissolve into a blabbering idiot! Julie, on the other hand, managed things like a zookeeper and never once lost her cool. She is younger, but on this night she was way more mature.

I'm a girl. Plain and simple. There are some things I just don't want to do. Guy things. This was definitely a guy thing. I wonder if I've been denying my inner Barbie my entire life. Actually, I don't care. There was an OPOSSUM sitting 10 feet from my bed! There was an OPOSSUM sitting on my new biking jersey AND on my kitchen table! During that whole time, where the hell was Ken?

POSTER

As young girls, Nancy, Barbara, and I shared a large dormer room. Being the oldest, Nancy had her own bed; Barbie and I shared a double. There was enough room for dressers, chairs, and a small table, which periodically served as a stage. It was in this room that we shared sister secrets, pulled pranks, and sometimes fought by digging our nails into each other's forearms. There was no privacy in that room and rarely did you feel any single item belonged to just one person.

On the wall between the beds was a cherished poster of the Beatles. It was row of head shots of Paul, John, George, and Ringo, taken well before the Yoko Ono days. Like many young girls of the era, we had our favorites and imagined meeting and falling in love with any one of them. Mine was Paul. He was by far the cutest and I would fall asleep under the poster imagining that he was singing directly to me.

Sometimes, using our hair brushes as microphones, we would stand on the table and lip sync Beatles' songs. "I Want to Hold Your Hand" and "All My Loving" were popular choices for this early version of karaoke. Many Saturday afternoons were spent in our room, producing concerts for each other and wearing out our meager collection of 45's. Containing easy lyrics that spoke of the promise of love and passion, these tunes were performed repeatedly on that small table and cemented my love of Beatles tunes.

This past week, I've listened frequently to Paul singing "Let it Be." It's on a disc of songs a friend made to remind me of my many gifts. The lyrics are powerful: "When I find myself in times of trouble, Mother Mary comes to me. Speaking words of wisdom, let it be." Hearing Paul's voice puts me in a reflective mood and I frequently cry when I hear this prayer to the Virgin Mother. No weeping, just a tear for the beauty of the music and the depth of the message. But as I listened more closely to the lyrics, I began to wonder if those simple three words were indeed a suggestion; or are they perhaps, a wish?

The question becomes more interesting when you learn that "Mother Mary" is not a reference to the Virgin, but actually to Paul's own mother, Mary, who died from cancer when he was just 15. The song was inspired by a dream in which Paul's mother came to him to let him know all was well. I imagine he awoke feeling that she remained a guiding force in his life and was keeping Paul in her care. What a wonderful image and one I consider often, as I imagine the watchful eyes of my own mother.

If the lyrics are a directive, they speak to the wisdom that many parents hope to pass along to their kids: Trust that you're in the right place. Trust your instincts. Trust that I have your back. It's the ultimate statement of faith and belief in a power greater than ourselves; in a parent that is gone, but still watching. In my own times of trouble, I rely on that faith to guide me to the next door, the next path. It's not always an easy task, because in those times of difficulty, I want answers and explanations, not reassurances. I don't necessarily want to know that at some point, all will be well; I just want to feel better that moment.

What if, instead, we hear those lyrics as a wish? What if the words are intended to be a confirmation of those hopes we hold deep in our hearts? Let it be. Let it be what I dream or desire. When I pray for others, let it be that their pain or struggle goes away. If the song is intended as a prayer, the power is in the faith that what we seek will be shown to us. Even if we can't see it.

I'm thinking it's both. I'm thinking it depends on whether we are listening, or if we are asking for something. If we are **listening,** the message is clear: "I got this, let it be"; accept this time and have no worries. But if we are **talking**, it becomes a request: "Please, let it be." For me, that's the struggle. The two collide when what I want is not what God has in mind for me. When I have to accept that in this moment, I'm exactly where I'm supposed to be. I'm on the right path, I need only to continue to move forward. Whether I like it or not.

I have absolutely no idea what happened to that poster of the Fab Four. I do know that I've been moved by music since I was that young girl standing on a small table singing into a hairbrush. Never did I imagine that the songs of my youth would continue to follow me into adulthood. Nor did I envision that music would continue to guide my dreams. I certainly never expected that at this point in my life I would still not be married to Paul.

REINING

When the local newspaper would no longer be delivered to my door because of the move towards an on-line edition, my first worry wasn't about where I would get my daily dose of news. No, my first worry was figuring out how I was going to manage my day without starting it with the "Jumble" Puzzle. Since the age of 10, I've read the comics with my morning Cheerios, completing whatever puzzle was available. Forty-seven years later, I have the same routine, only now Julie has hopped on the train and we compete to see who can be the first to unscramble the letters and solve the puzzle. The solution is a logical process of rearranging the letters until the word becomes evident. Trying to outdo each other adds a layer of emotion, as we tease each other for missing the obvious ones. Sometimes the words just pop right out, and, at other times, we are jointly trying to figure it out over dinner. In any event, it has become a fun distraction in our daily routine.

Balancing logic with emotion is easy when solving word problems or playing board games, yet not so easy when negotiating life. It's a challenge I have yet to completely master. This past month I've been given multiple opportunities to work on that very task: the opossum visit, needing a new car and a new phone, and this week, a minor health complication. Managing all of that while adjusting to the ever shifting hormones has been a bit like swimming through mud. I can see the logic, I can see the practical side of things; I've just had trouble grabbing ahold of it. Once again, life decided to present me with an opportunity to gain some perspective.

Last weekend I traveled to Columbus to watch my beautiful niece, Danielle, compete in a national horse competition. An accomplished equestrian, Danielle is built like a pixie fairy and as a young adult has continued her love of riding and competing. Converging on Ohio for over a month, accomplished riders from all over the country compete in a variety of events and styles. I like to think of it as the Woodstock of horse riders! Danielle is a "reiner." In this sport, the horse and rider work as a team to perform intricate moves, with the goal of "skillfully guiding" the horse to perform a choreographed dance. It requires the ability to control the power of the horse by simple leg and rein movements. Well, it's simple for someone of Danielle's skill.

I sat enthralled among 5,000 other spectators watching the talented performers. I quickly learned to identify the pros from the amateurs and how to know if certain required movements had been completed. The technical aspects of the competition were lost in the beauty of the sport...in the emotion. The riders seemed to be flying as they sped across the arena on horseback. You could see the joy and passion on their faces, feel the love they felt for their horses, and you could hear the sighs of relief when they finished.

As her aunts and uncles waited for Danielle to enter the arena, the emotion grew for those of us who love her. She had never performed in front of a crowd this size and we all grew anxious. Nancy could barely sit without her legs shaking and we all held our breath when Danielle's name was called and her music started. Having been on exactly two horseback rides in my life, I was more than impressed when my beautiful niece began her routine. I could see the concentration on her face as she focused on the requirements of controlling her horse, Chick.

A large chestnut stallion, Chick was beautifully groomed with his braided mane. I was fascinated with how her horse responded to subtle, barely visible leg and arm movements. These two creatures know each other well and had run this routine countless times. At moments, it almost appeared as if Chick knew what to do before getting the directions. While Danielle focused, I could almost see her trying to rein in Chick's passion and power. It was an incredibly delicate balance between the art and the science of the sport, between the logic and the emotion.

I am, of course, capable of turning any experience into a psychological exploration. It's recently been suggested to me that my brain operates like a carnival and I need to introduce more logic into the colorful chaos residing in my mind. My ability to feel and express strong emotion is, at the same time, my most endearing quality and my Achilles heel. I can, with very little encouragement, act on my feelings instead of the facts in front of me. I can see a road is a dead end, but part of me will still travel it, hoping there is an outlet. Even when I can logically see that a situation is not in my best interest, I'm pulled along by the emotions, the hopes, the wishes.

For the last several months, it has been these very things that have ruled my day to day functioning. Menopause has found me struggling with mood swings and over the top reactions. But if

Danielle can rein in a 1,200 pound horse, I can do this. If this tiny wisp of a woman can control an enormous animal with the pull of leather and a kick to the side, then I can learn to make the necessary adjustments to create a greater harmony of logic and emotions. Hormones be damned!

The most exciting part of Danielle's ride was watching her run full tilt across the arena. The strength and speed of Chick was evened out by the calm control of Danielle. As she sent the right signals, Chick came to a sudden, quick stop while sitting back on his haunches. It was an incredible movement that always results in applause. It was a powerful visual of the importance of off-setting emotion with logic; of balancing my heart with my head.

Danielle didn't win this event. Instead, she made huge strides in preparing for the next competition. She learned she can push herself further, take more risks, and trust her horse to do the same. Danielle discovered she can use her knowledge to express the strength of her passion and let Chick express the gift of his ability. I learned that I can do the same thing when my emotions begin to take over. I'm going to sit up straight in the saddle and position myself for the ride. I'm going to grab the reins and take off. Then I'm going to pull back.

WORDS

Another year without Dad. Another year of grief. Another year of talking to him in the car and in prayer. It doesn't seem possible. Yet here I am, two years later, struggling to string together the right words to acknowledge this day. I've started and stopped this essay fourteen different times over the last week. I've distracted myself by working on this book, baking bread, and watching the Browns play. Funny, each of these distractions actually makes me think even more about Dad. I keep looking for stories that celebrate his life.

I thought of how he was not a big man but he lived his life big. I thought of writing how much I look like him or telling the story, again, of how he brought Julie into my life. I started a piece on his love of comfort food and fine cuisine. I spent hours figuring out how to tie together the story of the bracelet I wear every day that Julie gave me and the bracelet she wears every day that belonged to Dad. I spent time sorting through my "Dad Box" where I keep his eulogy, prayer cards, and old photos. I stared at the two pictures I keep of Dad on my refrigerator and I listened to one of his favorite artists, Rod Stewart. Nothing was working. The words were not coming.

My favorite place to write is sitting on the couch, laptop balanced on my knees, the TV on for background noise. Behind me sits the piano with a picture of Dad. In some ways he's always looking over my right shoulder, offering his opinion. As I struggled to find my words, there was a constant tickle at my brain that I just couldn't grab onto. I sat quietly, thinking that Dad was trying to tell me something. Slowly the words began to form. Like fingers moving across a Ouija Board, the inquisitive message came to me one syllable at a time: Is...it...dark...up....there?

I laughed out loud and just shook my head at these familiar words. Really? Did I just actually hear that? I knew the words were coming from my heart, but they were almost audible. It was the same question that Dad asked whenever I did anything incredibly stupid. It was the question I answered only the first time with a puzzled look as each subsequent time the answer was the same: "Up your ass where your head is!" That man sure had a way with words. His words are one of the things I celebrate the most.

This second year of living without Dad was, in some ways,

harder than the first. At this time last year, I loved someone more deeply than I knew possible. Picking up the shards of a broken heart proved difficult as tiny slivers of all my other life losses were sifted together with this lost love. The emotional wounds were open and I was forced to examine how I approach relationships. More accurately, I had to figure out to leave them behind. I longed to hear Dad's voice directing me through the maze of unanswered questions until I realized he had given me the best advice years earlier. After all, moving forward from adversity was one of his specialties.

On the day my mother was buried, my grandfather, Henry, looked at Dad matter-of-factly and said: "She's gone. You have four kids to take care of. Get busy." We once talked about why he never visited my mother's grave and he smiled as he said: "Darlin, if I could stomp on the grave and your mother would stomp back, I'd go every day." He taught me that people come and go in this life and if we hang on too long we miss a world of opportunity. Life gets dark, but it's up to us to find the light. I didn't recognize then the power of his words, nor did I realize they would continue to speak to me. I am, after all, Mike's daughter, and so I picked myself up from the rubble and began to walk in a new direction with Dad's words as a guide.

For as long as I can remember Dad's advice was pretty simple: "Keep your head down and out of the line of fire." Or: "Just go about your business." My personal favorite: "I have no bail money." I rejoice at how he could cut to the chase and whittle things down to the bone. I remember his sarcasm and his ability to make even big problems simple. I applaud his wisdom drawn from years of experience, and I appreciate the smacks to my head that he could deliver with a simple question: "Is it dark up there?"

More than anything, I miss the sound of Dad's voice and the banter of our conversations. Fortunately, after 56 years of listening to him, I have lots of memories to draw on and it's through words that I can continue to stay connected to Dad. Today, I simply needed to remember his to find my own. Thanks Dad.

Susan Emmerich

SIMPLE

Three years ago, Julie made a simple choice in response to a request to register with a bone marrow registry. Sure. Get a cheek swabbed and give a phone number. For Julie, this wasn't a complicated decision. It took 15 seconds of her life and she was back to chatting with her friends. Actually, she didn't even remember the event and so when she got a call three months ago, she needed to ask those same friends to jog her memory. Another request from the registry: would she agree to some additional blood work as she was a potential match. Again, sure. This time it took more than 15 seconds but still not a difficult choice. When the next call came informing Julie she was indeed a match for a terminally ill woman, she didn't hesitate in agreeing to donate stem cells. At this point, for many people, the decision might begin to become more complicated. Not for Julie. For her, it continued to be simple: "I have something this woman needs. I can make more."

Friends and family have been shocked, impressed, even puzzled by Julie's donation. More than once, she was asked why she would choose to help someone she didn't know; why she would endure a week of feeling ill to assist a stranger. Julie was quick to say that she didn't understand the question. Rather, for her, the question was, "Why wouldn't I do it?"

Once my heart stopped bursting with pride for her selfless act, I began to reflect on how simple it is to impact someone's world. I'll be the first to admit that I make life much more complicated than it needs to be. My clinical background as a licensed social worker and overwhelming desire to explore life from every angle often finds me over-analyzing the minutiae of everyday life. For years, friends have rolled their eyes when an evening of camaraderie turns into a round of asking folks who they want in their life boats! It's a game that some friends feel borders on being psychotic. I'm very capable of finding deep meaning in a horseback ride or disposing of a wedding dress. I've been accurately accused of having a constant party going on in my brain. But when I strip it all down, my goal has always been to understand how our life experiences influence how we move through this world; what moves our souls. The answer to that question is really very simple: we are at our best when we are touching the lives of others with our gifts.

186

Besides Julie, I personally know only one other individual, not a medical professional, who saved a life. Several years ago, my dear friend, Patty, awoke to the house next door engulfed in flames. Not giving any thought to her own safety, she ran toward her neighbor's basement window where she could see children trying to get out. Breaking the glass, Patty pulled four kids to safety. Her response to her actions was the same as Julie's, "Why wouldn't I do it?"

Not many of us can actually save a life but often we may just save someone's hope. Yet, so many of us don't. We don't do the simple positive things that could impact someone in ways we may never understand or even know. It occurs to me that our gifts are truly gifts when we give them to someone else. Since we all know we could do more, what gets in the way?

For me, I'm guilty of thinking I don't have time. Seriously? I have nothing but time these days. Julie is, for the most part, self-sufficient and is no longer in need of my daily parenting. My job doesn't require extensive attention outside the school day. My family is healthy and I'm not in a relationship that requires nurturing. I have to believe that I simply don't pay attention to the small opportunities that present themselves to me every day; those moments to pay it forward.

A few possibilities come to mind quickly: giving blood every time the Red Cross comes to my workplace, buying hats and gloves (now on sale) and dropping them off at the women's shelter, using that coupon to buy an extra jar of peanut butter and putting it in the food donation box at my church. Others include shaking the hands of men and women in uniform that I see at the airport or in the Chinese restaurant, picking up an extra volunteer shift at the Ronald McDonald House, or engaging the check-out person in a conversation rather than just staring at them. Not even one of these requires much, if any, effort on my part. They're simple ways to- perhaps-ease the stress of people I don't know or maybe just acknowledge their value in my world.

Then there are those things that may require more of my time and attention, but will actually enrich my own life: visiting my aunt more often, taking Mom to lunch, forgiving past hurts, and embracing new opportunities. These are simple steps to spending less time focused on myself and feeling more grounded. I'm sure I'll continue to find deep meaning in hot flashes and mowing the grass, but just maybe, those insights will lead me to paying greater attention to those little moments of possibility. **That's** what Julie taught me this month, 15 seconds of her time led to the potential of years for someone else.

As another year opens in front of me I have but one resolution. Keep things simple. Do the simple things, take the simple route. I will start every day asking why wouldn't I do something and end it by asking if I did. I'll remember that the simple thing is often the right thing. I probably won't save a life, but then again, I just might.

APPLAUSE

Before I came to love roller coasters, I loved the "Rotor." Remember? It was the giant cylinder that spun so fast that riders stuck to the sides while the floor dropped away. When it stopped spinning, if you didn't throw up, you were certainly wobbly for a few moments when your feet hit the floor. If you were lucky, you could get back in line, dizziness gone, before you again went spinning.

I've been thinking a lot about that crazy ride as I reflect on all the changes and challenges of the last four years. I've survived divorce, Julie leaving home, visiting her birth family, and the death of my father. I felt betrayed by the aging process and had my heart broken a second time. Each required me to hold on when it felt like the earth was dropping off, and I suffered more than a few bruises.

The hardest things I've done in my life have come with a price. Sometimes that price has been physical, sometimes mental, and definitely emotional. But they've always been worth whatever the cost and have resulted in me being more open. more confident. I've done almost everything I set my mind to: white water rafting, zip-lining, the Warrior Dash, and two century bike rides. I rode a horse, visited the Jell-O Museum, and saw Paris. Yet, there is one thing I set out to do that has eluded me for a very long time, a goal I set three years ago.

I was watching a basketball game and during a commercial break, saw a well-toned athlete doing "clap push-ups." You've probably seen them. Incredibly fit people who do a set of full-body push-ups, clapping in between each one. They require tremendous upper body strength, are impressive to watch, and I found myself wishing I could do even one. How hard could it be? One push-up...clap... back down. I committed to more than one training program, worked with more than one personal trainer, and told everyone what I was attempting. I did push-ups on the wall, the kitchen counter, and the piano bench, in an attempt to build up my chest muscles while getting increasingly closer to the floor. I got very good at doing push-ups on my knees (known as girl push-ups) and managed to do 10 with a clap between each one. But each time I attempted even one full push-up, I collapsed in defeat.

I told a friend the goal was hard and she immediately and

sarcastically told me that I just shouldn't do it. I silently rationalized that this had been a stupid idea from the beginning. I gave up on the thought for months at a time as I trained for other big events. I completed another century bike ride, and went back to swimming laps until I could swim a mile. I thought about practicing nearly every day, but I found myself too tired, or too hungry, or too anything!

I began to wonder…what if I couldn't do it? What if it never happened? Was I a failure, weak, unaccomplished? Even though the answer was a resounding NO, my inability to reach this seemingly simple goal drove me crazy. I put the idea aside, picked it back up. I did push-ups in the pool, at my desk, and then didn't do them at all. Why was this so difficult?

One answer is simple. A clap push-up is damn hard! Professional athletes make them look easy because they are professional athletes! I'm pushing 60! My strength, like most women, is in my legs, which is why I can ride my bike forever. The upper body strength necessary for this task requires a lot of training, particularly when opening a jar of blueberry jam can be tough.

The other answer was not quite so simple and is deeply rooted in the damage caused by my marriage. In that spinning world of divorce, the bottom did fall out on my confidence, self-esteem, and personal power. I worked hard to get it back, clinging to that wall, and briefly lost it again when I gave my heart away to the wrong person. Those rejections had me convinced that I wasn't capable, or strong, or beautiful. Along with a bruised body image, my mojo was gone. But when a wise friend asked me what I needed to do to get it back, I knew the answer. Do the damn push-up!

I started over. I did the clapping on my knees; I again consulted the wellness coach at work and a friend who runs marathons. My nephews, Danny and Michael, said they could train me in an hour, until they actually saw my attempt! My friend, Sara, sent a daily text with only one word, "push-up." My cousin, Donald, gave me specific exercises to do and the willingness to provide weekly encouragement. First thing in the morning, last thing at night, found me on the floor. I didn't care about my form, didn't care how many I tried. I didn't care if my chest touched the floor. I concentrated on speed to give me the momentum to clap. I worried about breaking my jaw! Still, I got no closer. The goal began to take on a different feeling, the familiar frustration that comes with not getting what I desire.

I had fantasized about video-taping the grand accomplishment with Helen Reddy's "I am Woman" as the soundtrack. I planned to send it to all the people who made me lose confidence in myself, the ones who made me doubt my abilities. That idea, based in anger and hurt, began to bother me, and my attitude about the push-up began to shift. Was this something I was doing for me...or to prove a point to others? Did it matter if those few people knew the damage they had caused?

That's when it hit me. I don't need a damn push-up to own my power! It was an arbitrary benchmark, set by me to define my strength. Wow. Recovering from loss and pain has nothing to do with my upper body fitness and everything to do to with the resiliency of my soul. If I haven't learned that, then I deserve the fractured face that may be waiting for me. I got up from the floor and headed out for a bike ride. For it is on my bike that I am most at peace with myself.

I'm back! The last four years have been much like that Rotor ride and more than once I worried about slipping. But I survived without falling off, and I will survive the next person or thing that tries to break my spirit. This crazy life will continue to present me with moments designed to test me, designed to send me spinning. Still, my heart is healed, open, ready. I might stumble and might be a bit wobbly, but I'm getting back in line for the ride. My mistake is not in loving with my whole heart, but in not demanding the same in return.

Am I giving up on that clap push-up? Never. But I'm choosing to work on it as part of my overall fitness. I'm in training for a sprint triathlon, and a third century ride is only a few months away. When I do pull it off, it will be for me. In the privacy of my own home, I will give myself a well-deserved standing ovation.

SOULS

If you want great conversation, join a writer's group. Full of words and opinions, there's rarely a lag in the banter, and writers are masters at asking questions and digging for answers. Whether it is fiction, poetry, plays, or investigative reporting, words mean information, emotion and passion. I'm forever impressed by the talent I encounter during monthly meetings and challenged by the feedback and encouragement provided. That's not to say I've always liked the feedback, but it's helped me grow as a writer.

In a recent email exchange, a fellow member asked me to ponder this question: "What moves the souls of baby boomer women?" Whoa. Where to start? Having just seen a phenomenal black and white photo of a young rain-soaked Liza Minnelli wearing nothing but a man's sport coat on an empty road, my first thought was "freedom." The freedom to feel, express and love without abandon, to not wear make-up, to ignore the expectations of others, the freedom to move through life at whatever pace fits. Freedom.

Since good writers do research, I decided to pose the question to all the smart, older women I know. Simply put to them: "What moves your soul?" The responses were anything but simply put, as they came in the way of beautifully written thoughts and observations. Still, I was moved by the simplicity of the collective message: family, nature, and God.

Peggy is moved by the laughter of children and the sigh when she has finished a wonderful novel. Cher spoke of the smell of clover while lying on a blanket in an open field, and Mary mentioned her connection to nature. Karen recalled a beautiful red bird dotting the whiteness of a snowstorm. Barb was stirred by the unconditional love beaming from her granddaughter's eyes, and Dana described meditating under the night sky. Deirdre and Suzanne both spoke of God's love and random acts of kindness, with Anne adding the power of witnessing compassion. All were in keeping with what I know of these women, of what I know of their hearts. But it was Marilyn's response that moved *my* soul.

Having survived breast cancer with the support of family, prayer, and a great oncologist, Marilyn was brought to her knees by being diagnosed a second time. Her darkness was vast as she battled to have some sense of normal returned to her existence.

When she did indeed win round two, she found herself in awe of a presence and power that daily lights her path. Not wanting to sound cliché, Marilyn is keenly aware that every day is a gift and she wants to be invested in each one. She strives to be a better, bigger person, who sees and does good.

That's not to say Marilyn doesn't have days and moments when she takes her blessings for granted. But instead of being a gatherer of things, she now describes herself as a gatherer of wonderful moments. She has been cancer free for 16 glorious years and welcomes the sunlight of the day with hope and passion. What moves her soul? Being.

I was deeply touched by the wisdom of these women, by the depth of their experiences. I was moved by their words and ability to describe the intimate moments that define their lives. For the past four years I've attempted to do the same by sharing my stories and memories. In so doing I've realized that for me, the question is slightly different.

It's not only what moves my soul but also about what *drives* my soul. What moves it, is my longing for an intimacy that moves beyond words and is communicated by a touch on the arm or look. I want to once again feel that walking into a room matters to someone. I've only once in this life felt cherished, and I want to feel it again. Loving deeply defines me in a way that is difficult to describe and has cost me my heart more than once. I maintain an incredible hope that my heart will find a safe place to dwell.

But the fact is, my soul is driven by words; driven by wanting to know people on a deeper level, to connect in a profound way. I love asking ridiculous questions that prompt friends to reflect and share. I can't help but find meaning in experiences that are, I think, designed for introspection, like rope-climbing, bike rides, and card games. Each one presents an opportunity to learn something about how I move through this world, whether with fear, regret, or passion. Discovering this love of writing has opened my soul to a voice I didn't know existed. The world looks different to me now and I'm most at peace when I'm connecting to others through that voice.

When I saw that breathtaking photo of Liza, my first thought was of wanting to replicate it. I shared that wish with the same writer friend who first posed the question. His response was simple: "Just give *yourself* permission." I want to find a sport coat, a rain soaked road at dawn, and dance. I want to throw my head back in abandon and know that my soul is alive. And then I want to tell you about it…someday.

About the Author

Susan Emmerich is not a writer by training and discovered her love of words late in life. In her first career as a licensed social worker, she worked in the areas of family violence and adoption. When her own daughter became school age she made the leap to school guidance to take full advantage of snow days!

While having coped with multiple losses in her life, Susan did not really take notice of their collective impact until her first menopausal mood swing. It was then that she found writing and biking to be the best medicine for a wounded soul. She currently resides in Cleveland, Ohio and is still discovering miles of new bike trails.

Made in the USA
Middletown, DE
29 August 2017